A Girlfriend f(
Learning to Live
in Conscious Relationship

by
Julia Chi Taylor

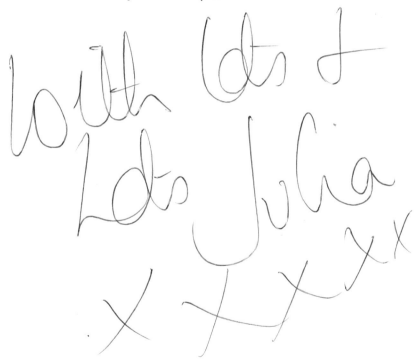

A Girlfriend for a Year:
Learning to Live in Conscious Relationship
Copyright © 2015 by Julia Chi Taylor
ISBN: 978-1-326-26297-6

Thank you, Ros Draper with all my heart. Without you I may never have found the love I yearned for.

'There is no coming to consciousness without pain. People will do anything, no matter how absurd, in order to avoid facing their own Soul. One does not become enlightened by imagining figures of light, but by making the darkness conscious.'

— C.G. Jung

Contents

Foreword

I was lucky enough to meet Julia at a press event over a decade ago, when I was invited to write about Imago Therapy for *Scarlet* magazine. Given my background in psychology, specialising in sexuality, I will admit to being sceptical about a 'new relationship therapy' that was 'recommended by Oprah'. However, upon arrival at the event, I was instantly struck by Julia's warmth and refreshing openness.

She led a room full of journalists through identifying our own patterns to help us understand the way in which we relate, sharing wisdom and her personal journey alike. When she introduced the Imago matrix, I was surprised to find that I could easily identify the roots of my own relationship issues, through re-framing my past in a simple, logical way. By the end of the session, I was more convinced than I'd expected to be, and my fellow journalists seemed similarly engaged with both the techniques and Julia.

As part of my feature, I had a session booked with Julia, to allow my then partner and I to learn ways to relate more effectively. Again, I was impressed by the methods she taught us to identify and work through our issues, and found that they helped me navigate the relationship more effectively (in this case, happily navigating away from someone who was clearly wrong for me and was unprepared to 'do the work'). Since then, she has become a friend, and someone I've recommended as a counsellor to many people. Her techniques 'toolbox', experience and subsequent empathy have been healing to everyone I've recommended her to.

When Julia told me that she was writing a book, I was excited that she'd be sharing her message with a wider audience. Though the spiritual aspect may not fit with everyone's beliefs, do not make the mistake of thinking this is a 'woo' book. Julia clearly explains tools that you can use to help relationships of all kinds run more smoothly. She illustrates this with her personal story in a way that illuminates the reality of 'conscious relationship', showing how the method can help overcome conflict, with others and within yourself.

I hope you find her words and techniques as healing and valuable as I have.

Emily Dubberley
http://www.dubberley.com

Introduction: Learning to Live in Conscious Relationship

I have been 'boy mad' all my life: I remember first falling in love at six years old with the curate's son. In 1982 I married for the first time – for keeps, I thought. I would never have imagined, as I'm sure few of us do, that I would ever become a divorced person. Yet I am now a divorced person four times over...

My journey of exploration through intimate relationship has been a lifelong quest to find true love. I have been in many relationships before, going in full of enthusiasm and hope, only to be disappointed both in myself and in the space I found myself in. In this journey I have learnt that true love comes from the inside out; that relationship is a mirror and intimacy the magnifying glass, and that in all the relationships and the loves I have journeyed with, I am the common denominator and that I can only work on myself and my own part. I have spent my life learning how to love and how to let go of need, of expectation, of insecurity and instead to accept myself and others and to listen and to validate the truth of another. Quite a challenge at times!

I have written 'A Girlfriend for a Year' to chart the beginning of a relationship and its unfolding, using myself and my own, 'real-life' relationship with my partner Anadi as the case study. The book is, on one level, the story of a relationship, and it is, I hope, an interesting story, but you would be forgiven for pointing out that I have been in relationships before, have indeed been married before, so why is this one special? Why is this one worth putting into a book?

My answer is that this is the first time I have felt able to have a really, truly, authentically conscious relationship. There is so much unhappiness in so many relationships, most of which start off with such promise. Often, people that have ended up in this situation are helpless, with no idea how it occurred or what can be done to improve things.

I believe there is a simple reason that many relationships 'turn sour', and I believe that being open to the possibility of truly conscious relating will not only mean less chance of unhappiness, but that it is the key to truly having a wonderful, exciting, healing, and lasting relationship with another human being. I would like to be able to help others realise this possibility.

This is the message of this book: that relationship is a place of healing if it is entered into with a commitment from both people to be conscious – to be 100% responsible for their 50% in the relating. This book is the story of my real-life attempt to do this with my partner, to stay conscious throughout all the ups and downs a relationship throws at you, however prepared you may think you are for it.

Imagine feeling so totally safe with another human being that we could explore absolutely anything, all the difficult stuff, all the stuff which isn't normally spoken of. Imagine if we could exist in a space of absolute clarity, where we were responsible for all our own reactions and we knew that the other was committed to the same thing. This space would become a space of absolute healing, interaction by interaction, creating an environment of safety in the space between two people.

I have spent my life in relationship, and within the exploration of conscious relationship, and, in meeting Anadi, I met a man who was committed to learning to relate consciously with me. Therefore, I shared everything with him. Processes that I could have worked on alone, I shared with him, so that he could learn to share too.

This was harder for him to do, as he was very practised at clearing his own 'stuff' by himself. If both of us were doing that, we could have missed the opportunity to go deeply into intimacy and clear the wounds from our past, where intimate relationship had not felt a place of safety at all.

I was keen to be totally transparent with this man. So I resolved to share everything, to teach him to help me heal me and for him to know me; and also to teach him how to heal himself and share himself with me. I did not anticipate weeks and weeks of struggling with the full commitment, but this had to be embraced, as it was what was happening...

So, as well as a story, the book is also intended as a guide to 'conscious relationship'. I have opened my heart and been entirely honest about all the ups and downs of my relationship with Anadi, in the hope that it can serve as an example of the many pitfalls and possibilities that a couple can come across while attempting to consciously relate with each other. I let you, the reader, into all 'the small stuff' – or the seemingly small stuff – the tiny dynamics that go on within relationship and that also come to define it. Our relationship situation is unique, obviously, as all are, but the emotions and issues involved are universally human.

Through sharing my own experiences and inner processes, I hope I can help you notice where the small things that arise within interactions can block a deepening of intimacy, and to be fully conscious in sharing this with your partner. I hope that you too can find the love that you seek.

What is Conscious Relationship?

Millions of people are looking for 'the one'. You may well be one of them. While there are different ways to enjoy relating with others, many people are driven to seek the traditional 'happily ever after'; an individual who can end all our searching, struggle and loneliness; the unique person we can journey on this planet with to help us make sense of the chaotic world we are thrown into.

We bond with people for all sorts of reasons. Sometimes, it is simply that we recognise ourselves and like what we see and feel when we are with this person. This is often how we form friendships and, unsurprisingly, we may meet these people because we are mixing with souls from similar beginnings and similar circumstances to ourselves. Within this mix, we may be unconsciously drawn to people who have similar sensitivities and needs – often from similar patterns of childhood 'wounding'.

The Wounded Child

Everyone has a wounded child within them. Even the most caring and well intentioned of parents won't recognise or meet every one of their child's needs – because they have their own wounds (and needs). This can be hard to understand as a child.

We come into the world incapable of surviving alone. We needed to be looked after, and so the adults – our parents and siblings, older family members, friends and teachers – are the authority figures that we look to for care. To survive childhood we try to keep ourselves as safe as possible, and relationships with our parents and carers form the foundation of that.

Relationships are a touchstone for us when we are very young, our rock to hold onto and make sense of this chaotic world. We are unconsciously shaped by the adults around us to adhere to what they think we should or could be, and are encouraged to hide (or emphasise) parts of ourselves.

The first seven years of childhood are key. At this time we are like little sponges. If, during this time, we are not heard or understood, our parents are impatient with us, or tell us that the way we think or do things is wrong, then we can become wounded.

How Wounds Happen

We are wounded when the adults around us, or our siblings or peer groups, are not able to completely take care of our emotional needs. We are wounded when we are not heard or recognised. We are wounded if we grew up hearing or witnessing anger or dysfunctional behaviour around sex; physical or mental abuse; addiction to alcohol or drugs. In many ways we all get wounded, though these ways depend on the child: what will wound one child may not wound another so deeply.

Perhaps a sibling being born when we are still very young changes our lives: the balance of power changes, the energy in the house changes, more attention is focused on the new baby, our mother becomes exhausted or depressed, our father takes control – or withdraws himself.

Maybe we learn that our own emotions are not valid, not acceptable: 'Don't cry' we are told, or, 'No, you don't feel like that.' We may have been shouted at, or laughed at, or teased when we wanted to get our message heard, or even worse. We may have been ignored completely by our family, and so shouted louder, or shut down our emotions.

So much can happen within a family home, and so many delicate balances that we rely on to feel safe can come crashing down around us. Relationships, our foundations of safety, start

5

to feel unsafe. We become disconnected and are hurt, 'wounded', within that disconnection. So we look for survival techniques.

I Will Survive

To survive, we adapt ourselves to make certain that the people we need to care for us keep doing so. If at any time we sense 'danger' (an emotion not approved of, the behaviour of a sibling threatening the balance, an event that caused sadness or loss to our parents and us, expressions of anger, or abuse) then we learn very quickly how to adapt and how to survive.

To adapt, we hid away parts of ourselves that seemed unacceptable. Maybe singing loudly in the house is frowned upon and so we hide away the lively expressive part of us, or lose the part that could be spontaneous. Maybe we grew up amid chaos and indiscipline and we adapt by being rigid in the face of it, or we reject the part of us that can be ordered and disciplined.

In order to stay safe, we lose, hide away and disown parts of ourselves, so that we might retain the love and attention of those that care for us. These adaptations are not all negative – they can help us too. They may push us to become an actor, a sports-person, a nurse: to become whoever it is that we are. However, they can also hinder us in our relationships unless we make the effort within the relationship space to consciously recognise and take responsibility for what makes us who we are.

Childhood Adaptations Within Adult Relationships

Our unconscious wants us to become whole, to heal our childhood wounds, and so will move us towards people and situations that are likely to give us the opportunity to do so. We will feel attracted to potential partners who mirror our lost and hidden parts, or who touch our wounds from the past.

Our unconscious attracts us to someone who is the best match for our deepest healing. It recognises the similar characteristics that we grew up with and thinks, 'This time I will get my needs met'. Our unconscious wants to finish the unfinished business of childhood, to become whole.

How we adapt as children is unique to us as individuals. While one child might adapt to being told to be quiet all the time by losing the ability to speak out, another might adapt by speaking up at every given opportunity. As adults, a couple might get together because they have 'complementary adaptations' such as these – where the wound is the same but the adaptation is different.

In reality, this can be confusing, and a power struggle can ensue, as each person pushes the other to be different, to get their needs met, to be heard. The irony is that this frustration can be rooted in the very thing that attracted the couple to each other in the first place: the hope of finding a similar soul and making sense of the world together.

You're So Childish!

When we react to a situation here and now, much of that reaction originates in the ways we adapted in order to survive in the past. A present situation reminds our brain of the past and says 'danger' to the body, which reacts. Immediately, the person is the child again, not reacting entirely to the current situation but projecting the past onto the present. No wonder there is so much confusion in adult relationships.

We project our memories and feelings from our past experience onto the present moment. In return, our partner may react in their way according to their own projections; and the here and now, the moment between two people, is played out according to patterns of childhood wounds formed decades ago. And so the cycle continues, and the wounds go deeper.

Because of our childhood wounding, relationships can feel very dangerous. Every time we fall in love, believing that this time this really is 'the one', within a very short time our adaptations can lead us to experience again the pain of disconnection and separation we experienced as a child. These wounds reside deep inside our bodies, and the body is like a child – it is uncompromising in its insistence to be heard. We may suppress our emotions and our pain through adaptations and distraction, or ease it through food, alcohol or drugs, but the body always presents its bill. It demonstrates where it is in pain from the past through reactions and drama in the here and now, leading to confusion within the present relationship.

Conscious Relating

However, there is something we can do about this. It is through disconnection that we get hurt, so it is through connection that we can heal. And it is in relationship that we get hurt and likewise in relationship that we can heal.

Most of what attracts us to another person is unconscious, which is why becoming conscious is vital for our healing. In doing so, the relationship can blossom and become the place of deep love, passion, connection and healing that it always has the potential to be.

When we 'grow up' we think we are adult, but in truth most of us are still carrying our wounded child within us, and that child reacts quickly to anything resembling danger from their childhood. True adulthood comes once we recognise that we must take responsibility and care of our wounded child. This means being mindful that every time our body reacts, a part of us is in the past. It is important that we press pause and release these feelings from our body, so that we can breathe and return to the present.

We are the only ones that can do this, that can be mindful of this, mindful of what we project and of what we put into the relationship space. This is how we create safe space between us and how we ultimately keep both ourselves and our partner safe. This is how we learn about true love, without projection or blame. But, in the words of Carl Jung:

'There is no coming to consciousness without pain. People will do anything, no matter how absurd, in order to avoid facing their own soul. One does not become enlightened by imagining figures of light, but by making the darkness conscious.'

Becoming Whole

We can all become whole by daring to look into the mirror of relationship to see ourselves, to see the parts that we do not yet love and the parts we have hidden, lost or disowned. Deep intimacy becomes a magnifying glass into ourselves and it can take courage to keep looking deeply within. But, with courage, we come to realise that finding 'the one' is not the end, not the answer to everything you are searching for: it is very much just the beginning.

If people in relationship together make the effort and the commitment to stay conscious throughout all the processes that play out, it may well be the beginning of a lifelong beautiful connection that few people on this planet have had the joy of experiencing.

Instead of keeping on looking for 'the one', we will seek within and clear ourselves. In doing so, *we* become 'the one'.

In the Beginning: Julia's Story

I have always been in love. I fell in love for the first time when I was six, and thereafter, there was always a boy that I loved. My friend Wendy and I would dream about the man we would marry, the amount of children we would have, the animals we would own. I believed in 'happily ever after' and would never have anticipated that my life would take such a hazardous route and that I would be married and divorced four times by the time I was 47 years old.

I believe that love is all there is. I have been curious about 'Love' since I was very young; I was privileged to be introduced to literature and poetry early and, through this, discovered that love and the quest for love seemed to be at the core of most people. I was originally brought up a Christian, and concepts such as the eternal love of Christ and 'Thou shalt love thy neighbour as thyself,' were teachings that influenced me deeply.

I have discovered that loving others truly comes through having nothing that blocks the flow of love. I have also discovered that most blocks to love come from within ourselves. I therefore have been on a lifelong quest to clear the stuff within me that blocks me from loving and accepting myself and, deeper than that, knowing my true self. From this place, love is all there is.

Around the same time that I started falling in love, I also knew that I wanted to run. From an early age, running and competing, succeeding and failing, getting injured then getting well and running free again have been an on-going cycle. This cycle gradually taught me to learn to let go of an attachment to an outcome – I learned that I was not a better person if I succeeded or a lesser person if I failed, but that I was just me on my own journey from birth to death. I ran internationally for many years and running at top level exposed me even more to my own ego and the need to let go. Running taught me that to be myself and know myself was all that was required.

I married young and, having watched my mother make a good marriage with my father, I attempted to emulate her. After ten years of my first marriage, however, I left and resolved to be true and open in my dialogues with men, with the words of my first husband – 'I never knew you, Ju' – ringing in my ears.

I trained as a counsellor when I was 32, having always been committed to exploring whatever arose within me. This gave me the confidence to be exploratory in my relationships with men – I had been using myself as a case study long before I wrote this book! However, I too-quickly assumed they were as interested as me in delving deep into relationship, and I repeatedly chose men who would not fully open, which both reflected my Dad, and of course the part of me that was not yet fully prepared to open either.

All of my working life, I have helped other people with their lives, from working for my coach in his fitness centre, aged 17, to creating a centre myself with my first husband; which progressed to personal training and evolved into counselling, healing, mentoring, coaching and therapy work, going deeper and deeper into helping others to heal.

I discovered early on that the essence of working in people's lives is the relationship you have with them, which comes primarily from the relationship you have with yourself. This is the essence of my philosophy, both personally and professionally, and along the running path.

Born to Run

I was born to run, and in the running step I discover myself again – within running I came to know myself at a young age. Running is within us all; almost all of us ran as children, and for me it is a place of expression and enjoyment. It has shown me where my imbalances are, both physically and emotionally, although I believe these are fundamentally linked anyway. If we are emotionally upset then physical movement is harder; if we clear physically then the emotions tend to arise and leave the body.

Running was joyous and free for me in the beginning, but the agendas and unrequited dreams of others got in the way. I internalised them, I brought them into myself, and so running lost its joy and became a place where I sought approval and love – and immortality, in that I was always striving for that 'zenith', the running times or results that would 'free' me and mean I had somehow 'done' my life and could be free to be me.

I discovered that I had it the wrong way round. I needed to discover how to be me again, to connect to my true self and to allow my running to spring from that. But as I journeyed towards 'freedom' I noticed that every time I became caught up in 'getting there', something would show up as an imbalance. And so it has been a lifelong journey to allow my running to take me where it wants to, and to connect to exploring destinations from a clear place within rather than a wounded place of hoping that running could somehow make me 'OK' and do something it never could.

Running has always been a metaphor for me, of both life in the bigger picture and my own inner landscape. I have explored all my imbalances and injuries from a holistic perspective and continue to do this as an on-going practice. I take full responsibility for the pain in my body, both physical and emotional, and approach whatever comes with an attitude of exploration and moment-by-moment attention to my own process.

Pointing the Finger – at Yourself

This philosophy extends of course to the relationship I have with myself and with others. I know I must focus on my own lessons, not those of the other, and if I find myself pointing a finger at another, then my commitment is to explore the three fingers that point back at me.

However hard it is at times, I take responsibility that the way I see things is not the absolute truth. It is simply coming from my own filter, which is why I endeavour to, 'clean and clean the mirror until there is no mirror to clean'. The essence of my approach to life, therefore, is that there is nothing else to do but to clear the stuff from my own wounds, clear my karma, clear my ancestral patterns, clear the beliefs that I have had imprinted and see what is left. My running, my writing and my relationships all rest on this one philosophy, summed up in three key phrases:

'Healer, heal thyself'
'Know thyself'
'To thine own self be true'

Happily Ever After?

All my life I had imagined the happily ever after: true love. Boy meets girl and a life of togetherness and sharing would unfold. However, I had been very hurt as a teenager, and had gone into my adult life unaware that the abuse I had experienced then would so deeply affect me and my relating as an adult.

I was a big romantic and had always dived into relationship with great hope and enthusiasm; I reflect on all the relationships I have had with men now, with understanding and love, and can see why I became used to hearing that I 'analysed too much', 'thought about things too much', 'hoped for too much', because the truth is I did.

My wounded self was hoping for the answers to appear in the arms of a man, and the lesson I had to learn was that the answers lay in my own hands. Although relationship is the place where we can all heal – in fact we are never not in relationship – it is in recognising ourselves coming up in the mirror of relationship that we must focus on our own growth, not that of the other.

However hard it is, we must come to the place where we truly see that the way we see things; our projections of the way things are, are our own. Only then can we enter into relationship recognising that the other is not the answer to our happily ever after, that we can keep ourselves safe by being connected to ourselves and owning what it is that we put into the space between us. We keep ourselves safe by communicating truly with another, and only then do we recognise that our work is to be the best partner we can be, rather than hope the other will be the one. Then relationship becomes a place of great healing.

By the time I was 50 years old, I had come to this place.

Learning From Experience

I have always been in relationship, I have been living with a man most of my adult life. I have loved all these men and I have come to recognise that we had done the best we could, we had loved the best we could love, we had committed the best we could commit, we had entered into relationship with as much truth and honesty as we possessed, and when the wounds had arisen and we had not been able to move into them and so heal them, we had instead moved apart.

I saw and understood this at 50 years old – and for the next three years I kept myself free from committed relationships. My life flowed with an ease I hadn't experienced before – not because I wasn't in relationship, but because I was more in relationship with me.

I loved my male friends. There were some I ran with, some I worked with, some I had occasional coffees with, some ex-lovers and partners who I sometimes met up with, and there were lovers too, who came and went, with ease – 'the orbiting men'. Then there was Tom, who orbited as well, and who I was 'into' and hoped for more - but overall I focused on deepening my connection with myself.

Happy Alone

I came to truly enjoy being alone. I came to a place where I acknowledged the longing for a deeper connection. I recognised there was much I had to express that was not being expressed alone – but I was also at peace with myself and my life. I accepted that having a relationship with a man was now not my path.

On December 6th 2012, I made my way to north London to meet Anadi, who was going to do a video interview with me on 'running as a meditation'. I called him from Seven Sisters as he had asked me to, feeling strangely nervous as I picked up the phone.

Anadi instructed me to catch the train to Bush Hill Park, where he was waiting on the platform. He had an ethereal quality. We hugged and then headed up the stairs and over the bridge to his car. He drove me home and went into the kitchen to start making tea while I took my boots off.

I stood in the doorway of the kitchen and Anadi turned round. I saw a flash of light, a flash of recognition, a flash of instant connection between us.

On 31st December 2012, we arranged our first date.

In the Beginning: Anadi's Story

I was the first born to parents that had been married a year. They had fallen in love young and married soon after. My mother gave birth to my sister Karen a year later, to my brother Stuart three years later, and things got progressively harder in the Taylor household. My parents divorced when I was five.

My mother, sister, brother and I moved around a bit before we settled in Harlow, Essex. This was a great place for me to grow up; I had the freedom I so needed to run riot in the woods. Swinging through trees, building camps and lighting campfires made for a great childhood and gave me the grounding I needed.

The one drawback was that, unbeknownst to anyone, I was slowly going deaf. My adaptation to this was such that it went unnoticed until I was so deaf that my pronunciation was getting harder to understand. After tests and visits to various experts it was decided that I needed an operation immediately, or my deafness would be permanent. My parents decided not to wait for the National Health and I was immediately admitted into a private hospital where the operation was successfully carried out. I awoke to a television program I had watched regularly but had not heard the theme tune to: Hawaii Five-O. I was so engrossed that I had it blasting at full volume with nurses and doctors rushing in to turn it down! I believe this is what 'turned me on' to music.

My father, who had a managerial position in a large travel company, often took us away on trips all over Europe. We had the privilege to stay in five star hotels and to learn the etiquette expected in those environments. My grandparents lived on Gozo, a tiny island near Malta, and we spent our summer holidays jumping off rocks into the welcoming Mediterranean Sea, swimming like fish. It was gorgeous: sun and fun, beautiful food, and welcoming people who became our extended family.

As I grew older, things became more difficult – I couldn't get to grips with societal expectations and so was always in trouble. Having got my hearing back I felt a sense of complete freedom and I became even harder to contain. I fought against discipline, my inquisitive nature taking me on adventures and escapades. My mother saw me as the man of the family and so there were expectations beyond my years and experience. This led to me fighting even harder for my freedom: a battle I now realise has fuelled most of my life.

Things came to a head when I was fifteen; I had a big bust-up with my mum and my dad arranged for me to live in a flat in London, on the condition I helped with the renovations, went to college and retook my exams. This was heaven. I got what I wanted: my freedom.

London: I Can Do Anything

I finished college having made some great friends and passed my exams. I had the realisation that I could do whatever I wanted; I really felt this to be true. I decided I wanted to be a musician. The experience of Hawaii Five-O had led me to being a music lover, now I just needed to learn to play an instrument. And, of course, find a job to buy all the equipment and pay my way.

I went to a job interview as a computer operator and programmer. I had a natural talent with computers, having programmed games for mates from the age of thirteen and found it very easy answering the technical questions that were asked. In fact, I realise now that I didn't even know at the time that I was being tested. But my enthusiasm shone bright and my talent for programming computers glowed even more brightly and when I got home from the interview, there was an answer-phone message saying I had the job.

Now, I had a flat in London and a great job that I enjoyed. I was learning to sing and to play the piano – I loved the sound and had friends that could teach me. I was enjoying life and enjoying my freedom!

After about three years I realised I could earn two or three times as much money programming computers as a contractor. I was now playing in various bands and was still financing my musical career. So, at the ripe old age of twenty, I became a contractor for Shell Oil. I excelled, so much so that they kept me on for three years. I learned to program on all their different mainframe systems and enjoyed learning the new technologies.

Programming computers is about problem solving and I loved the challenge. I also realised that my aptitude for problem solving was not only expressed through programming computers; I was aware that I had restlessness in my soul, and I needed to find out who I was.

When I was very young I had many experiences of leaving my body, which absolutely petrified me. I did my best to not sleep but of course this didn't work. I would regularly find myself 'outside' of my body, floating to vast spaces with other entities flying towards me. I had visitations and experiences of telepathy and the questions as to what this was all about needed answering.

I developed a keen interest in Buddhism and was delving into solving the 'problems' that were inherent in my childhood. I was devouring psychology books and all sorts of self-help books, and I learned to meditate and to be mindful of my thoughts. I realised there was a lot going on with me that was still rebelling from my parents and society, and my own investigations into this led towards taking drugs, starting with dope and quickly moving on to LSD and magic mushrooms.

My body is a temple? Mine was a full on rave!

Toward the end of my time at Shell Oil, the rave scene began. This could not have been timelier for me. I loved the music and I loved the drug ecstasy and the heartfelt connection all us early ravers felt while high; I was good friends with the original group of people that introduced it to the UK. They imported hundreds of thousands of pills and it was fun to be around.

I believe it was part of my growth to be involved in the so-called 'underworld' and the people importing drugs into the UK. My rebellious nature, my passion for breaking the rules, my fearlessness, my personal enjoyment taking the drugs were all vital ingredients that drew me to that particular world and the people in it.

Having worked in various recording studios all over London, I had come to meet followers of the Indian Guru, Osho. It didn't take long for me to fit in with this world – little did I know that Osho and his ideologies would become such a massive part of my life. The philosophies and meditations worked well with my investigation into altered states and the nature of the mind. Osho was all about being consciously in your heart and this had become my main focus with ecstasy.

I left Shell Oil and went to work at JP Morgan. This transition was easy. The contract with Shell had come to an end and JP Morgan needed people with my skill set. I decided to invest this money into a record label, Fokus Records, with a mate of mine. Our first release became a dance-floor hit. We had money pouring in, knew all the rave organisers and were a massive part of the whole scene. It was the most liberating time of my life – up to that point.

Ecstasy changed a generation. Thousands of people, all loved-up and dancing to the same beat was an incredible experience, and to be playing such a massive part, both with the music and taking the drugs, was beyond any dreams I had. This went on for a number of years with me as a record producer having hit after hit. Then it all went, as they say, 'Pete Tong' (wrong).

I woke up in the early hours one morning with the police everywhere in my flat. They had dogs and were not messing about. Everyone was arrested and taken to different police stations – except me. I phoned everyone I knew to be involved in the rave scene and realised, to my horror, they had all been arrested. I did my best to support their families and partners that had not been 'taken down'.

This was the beginning of a decline, though I didn't realise it at the time. Although I had not been collared myself, everything was about to change. My friends had gone to prison and things were no longer fun. My quest to know myself had become such a thirst I decided to leave everything and go to India. It was time to go to the Osho Ashram (a commune run by the guru) and get down to some serious meditation.

Life in the Ashram

During my time as a record producer, I had been involved with a number of women. I recognise that my role was an attractive position, for many reasons, and for me, someone not so confident at 'chatting up' women, it worked well. I had created a space where I didn't have to. Then I got to the Ashram in India and the freedom there was beyond any experiences I had as a musician.

'Do you fancy a date?' was the line that meant let's go out, grab some food and go and get it on. The novelty of this wore off quite quickly for me as it lacked the connection and intimacy I craved. I met a Tantrica and spent the rest of my time at the Ashram with her, learning and practising Tantra.

My meditation had advanced to very high levels with me practicing Vipassana (a way of self-transformation through self-observation, focusing on the connection between mind and body) for hours on end every day. I took workshop after workshop learning about myself, going deeper and deeper into my 'stuff', my fears, my reactions, my conditioning, my self-hatred and my anger. I realised this was one deep rabbit hole, but I was on my way to liberation.

Up in Smoke

While travelling in the mountains of India, I met an Indian man who owned a cannabis farm, and we arranged for him to drive kilos of cannabis down to the Ashram. I would pay him for it and then sell it at a great profit – ironically this paid for the expensive therapies and groups I was doing. I found it very amusing that my rebellious nature was actually paying for my spiritual growth.

I came back from India after six and a half months. I had deepened my inner journey, but I was completely out of money. I decided to 'get working' again. Once again, this was an amazing process; I loved being a part of the underworld and I loved having huge amounts of money coming in and not having to work for it. We imported over 2.5 tonnes of cannabis.

On one occasion our driver, who picked up the dope, was unavailable and I said I would go, 'just this once'. I took a mate, Paul, along for the ride, I appreciated the company and he needed to earn some money. Of course the inevitable happened: Customs and Excise were waiting for us and put us in a high security jail. Unfortunately, not being made of the same grit as me, Paul had a nervous breakdown. After seven months I took a guilty plea to save Paul from committing suicide. I never saw him again.

I was given a four and a half year prison sentence that I served mostly in high security prisons. Prison was quite a meditation for me; it really was like living in a monastery. I had food, shelter and the time to spend hours a day meditating. I worked out in the gym, smoked lots of dope and occasionally dropped some acid (LSD). I served about two and a half years of my sentence – it was a long time and passed quite uneventfully.

After my release, I flew to India, back to the Ashram. It was a great way to see in the New Year of 1998.

A New Album, a New Era

I set up a band and went on the road, spending thousands of pounds recording an album, which I am still very happy with to this day. I met a girl who was also a musician and also into spirituality. We journeyed together until she had a bad miscarriage. This was a very hard experience to cope with and we ended up parting ways. Amid the chaos that was this experience, the studio I worked and recorded in went bust and the band split up.

I was left with nothing. All the hard work and touring had brought me to a place where I really had to look at myself and what I was doing. I realised I had to make a change and decided I would go back to computers until it was clear what direction to take. Little did I know...

I very quickly learned how to create website pages and started to make some money. This progressed into me learning the new programming languages that had come into the IT world since I had left. Before I knew it I was creating small e-commerce websites and working with a graphic designer.

A good few years into this I landed a three month contract with a company that streamed video over the internet. Four years later we parted ways. I had learned so much about streaming

22

technologies and developing web-based software that my new direction had blossomed. I had already started to develop SoundsOrange (which grew from a Mind/Body/Spirit download site to being described as the Amazon of the new age world!) and was on my way to developing other software such as iMediaLibrary.

Meeting Julia

I had started to interview people for SoundsOrange as a way of generating interest in the website. I didn't want SoundsOrange to be all about selling MP3s. We now had concert videos and interviews as well as e-books and all sorts of free downloads.

Julia's PA, Amy, had emailed me to ask if I would like to interview Julia. I was not so sure about this as I had been told Julia was a runner: what was the relevance to SoundsOrange? I spoke to Julia and it became very obvious that she used running as a meditation: there was the relevance. I met Julia a Bush Hill Park Station. She looked very sexy and full of life.

'She's alright' I thought to myself. 'Better keep a professional head on here!'

We chatted away like old friends and almost ran out of time for the video. The interview went very well, it was great fun and we parted ways agreeing to hook up in the new year.

A few days later a small pendant with a hand-painted Pegasus arrived in the post with a letter written in left handed writing from Julia – we had discussed Julia's left-handed writing attempts in our interview – saying 'Spring well' (the Pegasus symbolises 'going forth'). I was really taken by this wonderful gesture. I knew we had a connection and it was obvious we both felt it. In fact I spoke to a dear friend of mine about it and it was obvious that I wanted to meet up with Julia again.

Not long after, I was helping a friend out streaming his event over the internet. I had set up and got the stream working, so I could relax a bit. I headed down and, in a crowd of a few hundred people, came face to face with Julia. I then 'knew' there was something going on here. We chatted for a while, before I had to check on the video stream. When I next saw Julia, she was on the dance floor with another guy – I went to say hello and got the 'vibe' from him that she was taken. I decided not to intrude, if she had a boyfriend that was that.

A few hours later I saw Julia come upstairs to the chill-out room. I saw her talking to a few people and noted that the guy with the vibes had disappeared. I went and said hello. Once again we chatted like old friends. I really liked Julia and, once again, decided we should hook up in the new year.

We were in touch by text and even wished each other a happy Christmas on Christmas Day. Julia was flying off to Barcelona to run a race and I was happy that we would meet up again soon. We stayed in touch by text. The communication got more and more flirty, and on the 31st December 2012 we arranged a date.

A Girlfriend for a Year Diaries: Part One

Friday 5th April, 2013. *'Something's going on for you. It's Tom, isn't it?'*

After our first date, things grew between us. Three months later, we were at Anadi's flat, having met to see a film made by a friend of his. We arrived with plenty of time to spare, had a coffee, chatted and queued up for the show. There were other acts on stage before the film, including Tom, who played some music and spoke.

Afterwards, Anadi and I went home to his flat and talked and made love until late. I woke up feeling churned up and tearful, with a huge desire to pull away and to go home.

'Something's going on for you. It's Tom, isn't it?' Anadi said.

'Yes' I nodded, the tears starting to flow.

My history with Tom wasn't, it transpired, quite yet history.

'It's whether you want to move on from him' Anadi said.

'I'm not sure if I do' I replied.

Tom and I had been 'hooking up' occasionally for nine years and my heart had been caught up with him all that time. What's more, he and Anadi were friends.

'I feel like I want to go home' I said.

'Well if you want to go home, beautiful,' Anadi said, with such love and compassion in his eyes, 'then you must go home'.

'But I know I must stay' I said – and I did.

I knew I must stay and stretch beyond the 'stuff' that was arising – stuff that meant that for me love was muddled up with people being absent and withdrawing and leaving me and not loving me. In moving towards Tom I was going towards what I knew, a place of 'safety' even though that place was filled with disconnection. Yet what I longed for was the connection and love Anadi was giving me; so I knew that my pulling away was what I think of as my 'stuff', my reacting to the past and not the present, my sense of this new, more connected relationship space not being safe – I was hesitating to dare to surrender to a deeper connection.

Throughout that day, my body and being alternated with such feelings of love and connection with Anadi, then overwhelming feelings of pulling away and running back home. But I stayed. I simply knew that this was what I must do and we had a lovely day, talking, eating, making love – all in his bedroom. We didn't get dressed until it was time for me to leave.

Sunday 14th April. *I Was Free*

Marathons have been my barometer, across all areas of my life. I could seem relaxed and free in my running, and then a marathon coming up would show me that there were areas of 'work' still to be done, my ego rising and convincing me that a fast time would somehow change my life and all my troubles would disappear. This myth at the core of my being showed me where I was not free, not conscious.

When Anadi and I had first met back in December he had interviewed me on the idea of running as meditation. I had said then that I would know if my running had truly become a meditation if I could run a marathon free of any attachment to an outcome.

Now Anadi was coming to watch me race in the Brighton Marathon. He knew I was still in touch with some of my 'orbiting men' and he was still working with his process within this, so deep for him, so hard, but so necessary. At the time I was more and more resolved to live my 'free life', and for me then, 'freedom' meant not being 'controlled' by anyone and relationship. It felt like a place of control for me.

All of my past relationships had ultimately felt suffocating, with the relating not being as conscious or as deep as I would like to go. With limits and boundaries and a lack of willingness on my partner's side to dive into the stuff that arose, I would feel restricted.

Because of this, on the Friday I had sent Anadi an email, trying to explain my feelings of wanting to pull away as the intimacy grew, of relationship not feeling like a place where I could be free. These feelings were obvious to both of us, and I was hoping to clarify what it was that I was experiencing. Unfortunately, the opposite happened and he misinterpreted it, thinking instead that I didn't want the relationship. He didn't answer all day, saying he was processing my email.

I didn't realise this at the time and went to Brighton to collect my race number and have a drink with my friend Si in his wine bar, which would later be hosting the after-race party for an ever-growing list of friends. I called Anadi later in the day as I wanted him to come down that night, rather than on the Saturday as planned. He told me he would come down but was thinking he wouldn't watch the marathon, or come to the after-race party, as he didn't want to meet all my friends when he was feeling the way he was.

It was my turn to misinterpret, thinking that he wanted to exit from the relationship.

'Don't come at all then,' I said.

I thought he couldn't handle me wanting my freedom and I knew I wasn't ready to commit. 'I understand. I get it, but let's stop now, let's not do this...' I said.

I thought there was nowhere to go and ended the phone call. I had a client arriving imminently, but still decided to call him back.

'Let's talk later,' Anadi said.

'I don't want to talk' I said, and hung up.

My heart was in agony, I was fighting back the tears and I had a couple coming to work with me in about three minutes... I called him back again. 'I will talk later.'

'Shall I come now?' Anadi said.

'Oh yes, yes, come now...'

The doorbell rang and my clients arrived. I worked with them for a couple of hours and very soon after they left, Anadi was there. I had the latest night in the run-up to a marathon I have ever had, but it was beautiful and connected and I was so glad he had come.

We had a lazy morning in bed on Saturday. My friend Greg was racing an Ultra race across the downs, and in the afternoon Anadi and I checked where Greg was on the race route, on their website. He had passed a checkpoint in good time, indicating he would be arriving in Jevington, just up the road, in an hour or so. We decided to drive there to see him run past.

We found refuge and cake in a little tea room, the sound of rain loud on the plastic roof, until we decided to brave the wet afternoon to make sure we didn't miss Greg run by. As he approached and saw that it was me, his energy showed real joy. He was running beautifully, confident and relaxed and full of grace. We hugged and then watched him turn left and run up the hill, homeward-bound.

We drove to the sports park in Eastbourne, drying my soaking clothes with the car heater as we went, and arrived just in time to see Greg race home to seventh place – looking fresher than you might expect from someone having run 50 miles. It was a happy afternoon. Looking back at this time offers such good memories. Anadi and I were so close and so connected, totally in love and totally at ease in one another's company.

My own race day dawned. I was very relaxed. The only glitch in my energy field was an awareness of my slightly weaker left side. Otherwise, calm was within me. I arrived at the start line with no attachment to outcome, ready to take one step after the other. A meditation on the move, as I had said in that first interview with Anadi. And I ran that way. In truth, I loved the run, even though the wheels metaphorically fell off at 20 miles. But then, I hadn't done the training required. At 22 miles I said to myself, 'it's OK – you never have to do this again', and it was with real resolution and peace within, not from a place of angst and pain. I surrendered to the moment and felt a falling away of an old out-dated pattern.

I was free.

The afternoon was wonderful – Si, Debbie, Jane and Anadi were at the finish. We all went to Si's wine bar and twenty or so friends joined us for food, drinks, fun and deep friendship.

That night my stomach hurt and I was still awake at 3am, but fortunately I was only working during the morning the following day and so on Monday afternoon Anadi and I lay on the bed and talked and made love. I still felt resolved to be free. I had unfinished business with Tom and I wanted my freedom, but I loved Anadi deeply.

'I will do this' I said. 'Sleep with other men. I am going to do it. I have to be free to live my life as I want.'

'OK,' Anadi said. 'I know this and I am with the programme, but I want to ask one thing.'

'OK,' I said.

'Will you stay with me in the process with it, and support me through whatever occurs?'

'Of course I will...'

Tuesday 16th April. *He went, as he always did, until he came back again...*

Following his performance before the film, I'd emailed Tom, saying it had been good to see him. We'd been emailing back and forth a bit and it was evident he was opening to meet up. This was usual in our pattern of relating: the orbit would come round and I would feel when it was due.

Now, he was suggesting coming to see me at the weekend. I hadn't seen him since December, before Anadi and I had started our relationship. I knew I wanted to see him, but before I replied, I wanted to let Anadi know. I called and got his answer-phone. He was on a train going to a meeting, so I texted him. He received it just as he was going into the meeting: what timing! But he replied saying he felt OK about it. I replied to Tom and we arranged for him to come over the following Sunday evening.

Anadi called me at lunchtime and very quickly said, 'I'm OK man, I feel clear.' We agreed to talk later, and did so for a long time. I felt tense: a fear of loss, a fear of being told I was wrong, a fear of hurting Anadi. But I could also feel that he was clear, genuinely clear.

On the Thursday I travelled to Devon with my friend Jane to see her amazing art installation. The change of scenery and connection with Jane made for a lovely evening, and the enriching conversation and her incredible artwork took me deeper into my own self-trust. Anadi and I were in touch all the time and, as always, our relationship grew deeper and closer as we were open and truthful with one another.

On Sunday, Tom arrived. I loved him the moment I saw him. It had always been thus. But throughout my time with Tom I kept Anadi in my heart, and I kept in touch with him too. I told Tom about Anadi, that he was cool with us hooking up.

'Of course,' he said. 'He's an Osho man.' (Followers of Osho, Sannyasins, are connected and integral with 'free love' and express that love sexually and with different people without possession or necessarily being in a relationship.)

We shared and caught up. He wanted me to hear some music he had made, so we went to his car and drove along the seafront and up onto the downs, the moon hanging in a starlit sky with wispy lines of cloud streaking across the night. We drove without speaking, and the music filled the car and the night and the space between us. Our connection felt true and at peace.

When we came home I gave him a massage which ended with oral sex. We lay talking afterwards and he told me stories. I left him to sleep on the healing bed in my therapy room and went to my own bed. In the morning I gave him coffee and a croissant and we talked some more. Then off he went, as he always did, until he came back again.

Monday 22nd April. *We Were Closer Than Ever*

Anadi and I talked and talked. I felt my heart open more and my love for him grow deeper. The week went by and it was clear that there was no damage to our relationship through Tom's visit. The truth seemed to be that we were closer than ever.

Monday 29th April. *I knew we would not be meeting like this again.*

The following weekend proved to be evidence of this. On the Saturday evening my friends Rob and Maria came over for Anadi to do a video interview with Rob about his Tai Chi. Afterwards we ate, drank and had a jam session: Anadi on guitar, Rob playing violin and Maria and I singing – a truly amazing evening and after they'd left, with the video equipment still set up, Anadi and I filmed ourselves making love.

All Monday, I could still feel the magical connection that had deepened with Anadi over the weekend. My love for him felt limitless and expansive.

Tom and I were still in touch, and he asked if he could call by later that day.

'Of course you can,' I said.

I was busy working, but knew I must tell Anadi before Tom arrived. A tiny part of me played with the idea that he could come and go and Anadi would never know but I knew this would not be good for our growth, or mine.

I called Anadi, and he was not happy. He didn't know how I could see Tom so soon after he and I had been together – he was still loved-up from the weekend.

'So am I,' I said. 'Nothing has changed about how I feel for you but I have to do this. I know I have to.'

Tom arrived, and we talked and ate. I kept in touch with Anadi. Tom and I had oral sex again. I went to bed quite early as I was getting up at 5am to run with Greg, and called Anadi. He wasn't happy.

'I know why I had to do it,' I said. 'I'm not in love with him any more'.

Anadi didn't hear me at first and there was a flash of anger from within him, which I totally understood. The flash subsided and we talked until 2am. At 5am my alarm went off and I ran 11 miles with Greg in a slightly altered state.

When I returned, Tom was doing Tai Chi. 'I felt you returning,' he said. 'And then you walked through the door'.
I showered and was standing in my pants in the bathroom, putting on my mascara, when he was ready to go.

We hugged, and as he went through the door, he turned back and we looked at one another. I believe it was then that I knew we would not be meeting like this again.

Saturday 4th May. *It was a happy hazy night and I was free*

I arrived in London in my blue dress, to see a show with Anadi. We met, and hugged and kissed in the street. It was so good to see him. We had time for a cappuccino before the show, and were sitting outside in the evening sun, sipping our drinks, when I told him I had nothing on under my dress…

The show was excellent; a sad love story – or 'not love' story, as it was unexpressed, unrequited. The music was great, I loved the lead guy's voice, the song he sang strumming his guitar, and Anadi's hand on my bare thigh throughout the performance.

After the show, we drank cocktails and ate supper in a small restaurant and Anadi gave me a ring with a beautiful purple heart-shaped stone and a blue star. The underground was closed by the time we decided to head back, and so we got a cab to take us all the way home to bed. It was a happy, hazy night and I felt free.

Monday 6th May. *I didn't tell him I was going with Anadi*

Tom remembered my birthday unbidden. It had never happened before. I usually heralded my birthday, or reminded him on the day, but this time I hadn't mentioned it and there in my inbox was an email with the title: 'Birthday'.

He was wishing me a happy time. He was heading for the mountains in Wales, so was uncertain about whether he'd have an internet connection. I thanked him and told him I was going to be in the mountains too: the Atlas Mountains in Morocco. He said he thought I would love it there. I agreed. I didn't tell him I was going with Anadi.

Wednesday 8th May. *Silhouetted in silence and in love*

The night before arriving in Morocco, Anadi and I shared a night in a hotel. We fell out of bed at 4am and were checked in to our flight by 4.30am. A few hours later we stepped out into the humid, balmy heat of a dusty Marrakech airport. My PA, Amy had arranged a car that took us into the mountains. We were delivered to the front door of our hotel and shown to our room, then up onto the roof terrace for a late lunch of tzatziki, omelette, bread, honey and sweet mint tea.

That night I woke up at 3am and stood out on the balcony. The moon hung in the sky and the stars were so bright, the mountains sat silhouetted beneath them.

'Are you awake?' I whispered.

Whether he was when I asked or not, Anadi joined me on the balcony. We leaned on the wooden balustrade and looked into the night and up at the stars, silhouetted in silence and in love.

Saturday 11th May. *There are points in our life – this way or that? – which completely change our direction*

The hotel owner, Abdul showed us a mountain route that he said, if hiked, could take six hours. We planned to run it, so he gave us food for a picnic, two bottles of water, and a map, and directed us up to the village, which was the first destination on our journey.

It was hot, about 37 degrees, and our hotel was already at 1,900 metres, so once we were through the village, alive with people, goats and donkeys and onto the mountain road, both Anadi and I felt the altitude, the heat and the very steep climbing.

It didn't take us long to settle in, though, and we wound our way up the hairpin bends of the mountain climb.

We took it in turns with the backpack, and a sense of timelessness descended. We'd set off at 10am and had no watch with us so we just took one step after the other, the mountains around and the villages below expanding before us. After we had been running a while we happened upon a café. Two men in long dark robes showed us a sign that told us that were at Tizi and the altitude was 2,300m.

We sat with them drinking orange juice and honeyed tea, and I bought a cobalt necklace. They cautioned us that the mountain soared up to 3,000m and was a hard climb. We thanked them and on we ran. We were feeling good in our bodies, relaxed and strong.

Unbeknownst to us, within another few miles of winding our way up the mountain we missed the road that would have eventually looped us back to home on the route Abdul had shown us and instead headed off on an extraordinary adventure.

As we rounded a corner a group of four little boys joined in and ran with us, one with a soul as old and wise as the mountains that we were running in; another with running in his being, matching our pace stride for stride beside us, his face beaming. The road came to an end, the boys scattered away and a group of men directed us over the mountain. Not speaking the language meant we didn't know where they were directing us, but looking out over the vista it appeared we were doing a big circle and we thought we could see where we were on Abdul's route.

The mountain took us up and up, and the terrain changed, the footing uncertain, a steep drop to our left. I had my first taste of re-entering a place of fear that had last taken hold of me on the side of a glacier in Switzerland during a race I was covering as 'roving reporter' for *Running Free* magazine two years before. My role had involved running a race a month around the world and

35

reporting on it. What I didn't know about that race was that two miles from the top we had a mile to navigate right on the edge of the glacier, a narrow rocky path with a sheer drop of thousands of feet to my right. I get vertigo when I am high up and can see the possibility of falling to my death: a sinking feeling in my lower gut that is immobilising. When I'm in these situations, I always think of Bear Grylls, who said that to climb Everest you must keep moving and keep taking small steps. Faced with the sheer drop on the glacier, I froze, but there was no one ahead or behind me nearby, so I used Bear Grylls's advice while clinging to the rocks on my left. The half hour it took me seemed interminable and for days afterwards I would have flashbacks to the incident.

On the mountain in Morocco, with some difficulty, I remained mostly in my centre, though nearly span out on a few occasions. Soon, we reached rocky terrain that was hard going and arduous and oh so high up: 3,000m by now, with sheer drops to the left and right. Periodic blue dots on the stones indicated we were on a tried and tested mountain route.

Dizzy with altitude and hunger, and with both our water bottles empty, we found a mountain stream and filled our bottles. 'We have the mountains within us now as well as all around us,' I said. We didn't know what time it was, but the sun indicated it must be beyond midday. We'd likely been on the road for three hours: food and a rest was needed.

We unpacked our picnic. Abdul had given us bread, cheese, tuna, tomatoes and two oranges. As we sat eating, an old goatherd appeared. We greeted each other and I offered him water. He sat on the rock for a while and drank from our bottle. I gave him an orange which he put in his pocket. He thanked us, pointed to the top to see if we were heading there and went on his way. We followed him shortly after and then joined him higher up where he was watching his goats jumping about the mountain. Their agility and sure-footedness inspired me. He shared a cup of his honeyed tea with us and on we went.

We could see the path we needed to join and headed across to meet it. But the mountain here was dropping away, and, as we started across it, my foot slipped and fear gripped me again. There was nothing but rocks, scree and a steep drop below. The power of the mountains overwhelmed rather than inspired me. I was immobilised again.

Anadi was still and patient as I sat on the mountainside and cried, then re-centred, knowing there was nothing for it but to inch my way to the path. I was holding on with both hands and almost going down on my bottom, when the goatherd suddenly came jumping and leaping across the rocks towards us. He gave me his staff and took my hand, and I let go. I surrendered, totally trusting him, and down the mountain we sped. At first I was totally terrified and then suddenly something shifted. I laughed out loud and shouted to Anadi, 'I feel like I'm flying!' He was leaping alongside, confidently finding his footing and using the shale like snow, when skiing, as a brake (he told me this, I have never skied). We finally reached the path.

I thanked my guardian angel deeply from my heart and soon we headed down towards the firmer road. There was still a rocky steep descent to navigate, but the shift had happened and I became more like a mountain goat than before. The fear seemed to have gone. A profound change within me had occurred and I felt lighter; I had needed to put my total trust in the man who took my hand. In both trusting and surrendering, the fear lost its grip and my spirit was able to fly free within my body.

We reached the road, and, after tipping the mountain out of our shoes, we started to jog along the winding, sandy path that was – we thought – now leading us home. As we ran, we passed groups of children on the road, women walking, carrying bundles of grass and men walking or just sitting on the path looking out at the mountains. A truck taking people home from work passed us by in a cloud of dust and, having dropped two people off, we decided to approach it to check we were on the right road. It seemed we were not.

We established eventually that to reach home we needed to cut across the valley and over the mountain. Three little boys were close by, fascinated by us and the situation, as we explained it to the men. We soon established that they would take us through the valley. We gave the older man 20 dirhams (about £1.50), he gave the boys some coins and we were off. Down a steep slope – thank goodness for my newfound confidence – down, down we ran, jumping over rocks down a narrow wooded path until we reached a river. We jumped, 'Famous Five-like' on the stones to cross it, then carried on up the steep slope that brought us up the side of the mountain. The boys decided they had taken us far enough and waved their hands vaguely up the mountain: 'Imlil, Imlil,' they gestured.

Anadi and I were alone again, and once again off-road on the side of a steep mountain. The views were awe-inspiring, when I dared look at them. A steep drop to our right meant I rarely did! But I wasn't as scared as before and felt good.

The air got thinner again and the terrain steeper, until we arrived at the top to a scene that remains etched in my being – the plains to our left looking like the Wild West, and to our right mountains rising in rocky granite magnitude. Which way to turn? There are points in our life – this way or that? – which completely change our direction. We had no clue. The route to the right seemed to be an established one, with red dots at intervals on the rocks, and so we chose to follow them.

I saw how changed I was, because the route was rocky and steep and at times very slippery with sheer drops but I carried on, fearless. The dots gave us a sense of security, so each one we saw lifted our spirits, but unbeknownst to us sent us further from our path. We found a boy with a scythe by the river and asked him the way to Imlil. He gestured up the mountain, back the way we had came. We should have turned left, it seemed, not right.

Anadi and I re-grouped. He noticed that the sun was dropping behind the mountains. We had run out of food and water, so found a stream, filled our bottle and started back up the steep, rocky mountain, but we were both low in blood sugar.

'I'm not safe to do this,' I said.

Anadi agreed that we were both too 'spaced out'. With the sun setting we thought it best to keep heading for the village and the road we could see above us, and take a long route back that at least was off the mountainside.

If we had water and firm footing we knew we would survive, but with darkness not that long away, being on the side of a mountain didn't bode well.

An executive decision made, we continued to follow the red dots that led us up to the village again, with a terrifying last rocky ascent. The road was red and dusty, and although we knew we were now taking the long loop around the edge of the mountain, we also knew that only time and a steady forward motion would bring us home. The sun was dropping in the sky, and as we wound our way down the red sandy road a sense of endlessness descended on us.

The people we passed smiled and we said *Bonjour*, which was understood without any real common language. The terrain changed and prickly pears now lined the sandy path. Three men appeared carrying a log, and a girl with magic in her spirit leaning against a tree assured us that the town we were heading for, where we hoped we might find a taxi, was down this path. We had no food and our heads were spinning, but we jogged on in companionable silence, united in our mission and sure that we would now live to tell the tale. Another rocky incline and we met a group of men and a youth loading up a donkey carrying cement in its saddle bags. The youth ran up beside me and took my hand to get me up the rocky pass.

The road wound on and the sky was turning purple with the setting sun, as we rounded the corner into a village and a shop, just about to shut. We bought biscuits and chocolate, devoured them eagerly, and our heads started clearing. The man we bought them from said that the place with taxis was 10k away – so about an hour, I thought. We had water and it was warm. I knew that even though we were on a road, it was rocky and the sides still dropped away. If darkness fell and we hadn't reached the village with taxis, we would need to stop and walk, and if necessary stop completely and stay and sleep until the sun rose.

Having decided this, our only concern was that people would be worried, but we knew we were safe. It seemed we were miles from anywhere, with the mountains rising and enclosing us on either side and the road, seemingly never-ending. The phut phut of a moped coming up the hill towards us on the deserted road was the only sign of life. It passed us, slowly, and Anadi called out 'Excuse sir!' The driver stopped a little way up the road and we established that we needed help, a taxi. He phoned a friend, and after some negotiation as to whether we had money he said his friend was coming for us.

By now, darkness had fallen completely and my thoughts kept moving to Abdul, who was expecting us for dinner. I moved those thoughts back to focusing on the here and now, knowing that we would appear, and that if he had worst fears they would not be realised; but I still felt for his worry over the lost English couple who he had sent out to the mountains that morning.

Our latest guardian angel, without whom we would have been well and truly lost on the mountain, stayed with us. After a while he motioned to us to climb aboard his moped and I once more faced my fear – no control on a steep, slippy mountain path with three on a moped. I clung round his waist, Anadi held round my waist and after a few bends where my heart was in my mouth, I closed my eyes and once more trusted a stranger on the path.

Headlights were coming towards us: our taxi was arriving. We deeply thanked our moped man and gave him one of our 20 dirhams. As the taxi sped down the mountain, we saw how far we still would have had to go to reach the town with the taxi and how far we still were from home.

We reached the village of Imlil at 10pm, twelve hours after we had set off. Our driver didn't know the way to our lodge and a group of men gathered. It was established who we were and Jamal, the owner of our lodge was called to say that we were safe.

It was then that Anadi and I realised that there was general widespread relief at our arrival. The men in the village climbed into the taxi with us and came the last mile to deliver us to our front door, where we emerged dusty, exhausted, and transformed.

Understanding the Process:
Power Struggle and 'Stuff'

If we are completely clear and at ease, whatever another human being does or says does not produce a 'reaction' within us. That is, we never move into an angry, defensive or confused position. In reality, most of us do so at some point, particularly if we feel vulnerable.

When we 'react' to another person, it is because they are showing us parts of ourselves we have hidden away or lost, forcing us to deal with them. The reactivity we feel in the present has an arrow pointing to pain from the past; pain that hasn't been cleared or healed – much as my mountain 'adventure' involved facing fears of my Swiss experience.

During the early stages of our relationship, Anadi and I faced various fears. Our own adaptations meant facing power struggles within ourselves and within our relationship.

If You Can Feel It, You Can Heal It

How we react, our reactivity, points to what I call our 'stuff', and this stuff that we carry around with us is like the scar tissue around our wounds. We react to 'protect ourselves', which feels the safest thing according to patterns picked up from childhood. However, in truth, if we own our stuff we can know that when we react, it is a signal that there is work to be done.

One example of this was my reaction in the mountains. I have an idea that this vertigo accesses a deeper fear within: fear of dying, fear of living, fear of relationship/ love/ intimacy. I see these three things as continuous and believe that most humans are carrying fear. My sport and my adventuring access this on the physical level and bring it up for me to release, allowing me to go deeper into life and relationship without fearing death.

I am on a lifelong journey to free myself from fear. As a child, I learned in the gospel of John: 'There is no fear in love, but perfect love casts out fear. For fear has to do with punishment, and whoever fears has not been perfected in love.' My life's journey is to live this.

Press Pause

At the core of most people's being, lies fear. Reaction springs from fear. When we are reactive – which is a very different feeling to intuition – it is important to press pause.

Feel the feeling in full.

Resist attaching a story to it.

Drop between the spaces in any thoughts

Feel the sensation in the body

Then we can simply allow the feeling, the pain, to clear. In doing this, it helps us stay in the present and work with what is actually occurring, rather than operating from the past.

I have noticed, in working with people and within my own life, that the 'issues' in a relationship often show up very early on. These issues, where tension or irritation arises can initially – especially during the 'honeymoon' phase – be ignored, brushed over, even looked at with fondness.

Indeed, often the very thing that is an aspect of endearment early on becomes a real 'bugbear' as the relationship progresses. For instance, someone may be jealous or possessive and initially this can be received by the other as a sign of being loved or of being important and later becomes a source of contention.

Who's the Boss?

When the initial romantic phase passes – this can be anything from three weeks to three years, depending on the couple and circumstance – then a power struggle can ensue, which can last for the rest of the relationship. The same dynamic can play out again and again, limiting growth and limiting the deepening of intimacy; or maybe a couple break up; or maybe they end up leading parallel lives.

The power struggle is essentially the inner child hoping to get their needs met. The unconscious plays a much bigger part in relating than we recognise when we are attracted to someone. Perhaps both people felt unlovable or unimportant in childhood, and their complementary adaptation is that one person would act out being possessive or jealous, whilst the other would pull away – and so the power struggle is set up. One person definitely gets to know they are wanted by the other acting out, but ends up feeling suffocated, and so the experience of 'being wanted' isn't healing or healthy. The other continues feeling unwanted or unimportant once the person pulls away, and so they end up reliving the wound, and keep pushing for attention.

Deeper dialogue and conscious relating can heal all this, which I endeavour to demonstrate through sharing my story. In my relationship with Anadi, I initially wasn't able to commit, to stay truly open to our dialogue and dynamic and to fully hear what was going on for him. I had to work through feelings of 'being wrong' for doing something out of the societal norm, and also because it accessed a core childhood wound within me of 'being wrong'. And he had his own feelings to work through too...

Anadi's Perspective

Many people in relationship have needs that they expect to be fulfilled by the other person in the relationship. These 'needs' can have a tendency to block intimacy. Any need projected onto another creates a condition on love or connection, and if there is a condition there is a limit to intimacy. 'If you are not fulfilling the need I have then I will close down and withdraw my love' – this is prevalent in so many relationships, sometimes in very subtle ways, sometimes not.

My experience, generally, of people in polyamorous relationships is that they have intimacy issues and by having many partners avoid intimacy (of course, there are a select few who do not have these issues and enjoy deep intimacy with many partners). Having lived in various Ashrams (Indian spiritual communes) and experienced 'free love' I was aware that my preference was to be in relationship with another and to be intimate with the person I was in relationship with and no other.

Julia's desire to explore every dynamic that went on in our relationship and for us to have intimacies with other partners was not my first choice. I felt there would be a limit to our intimacy if others were involved. I felt I would not be able to fully open knowing that Julia was seeing other men.

This raises a very poignant question: if we are in an open relationship, what right do we have to place 'demands' on the other? Our culture seems to be of the opinion, generally, that sexual faithfulness trumps everything else. If we are sleeping with other partners, what right do we have to ask, for example, 'why didn't you call when you said you would?' The answer is, of course: 'we are in relationship'. The context of the relationship is irrelevant; relationship is all about relating and relating is all about connection. This is true right across the board, whether the relationship is between friends, siblings or lovers – be there one or many. If we agree to go into relationship with others we agree to a level of relating. The level of relating can get a bit blurred and of course this can lead to the breakdown of that relationship. The answer is to be clear about each other's expectations, and this way there is no confusion or disappointment.

Julia was very honest about what she wanted, she was very clear about her expectations and so I had a choice. I was empowered by Julia's clarity and the fact that we could talk about and investigate our relationship. By deciding to 'be in it' I then had to honour the 'deal' Julia and I had agreed to.

Having met Julia and spent more and more time with her, I realised that what we have is not of the norm and is very special. We shared a deep connection, like no other I had experienced, there seemed no boundaries to the depths of intimacy we were diving into. We truly love each other and this was obvious for all to see very soon into the relationship – friends and family commented on our togetherness regularly.

When we were together nothing else in the world mattered; time ran its own race and often sprinted past us. When we were apart the connection between us remained, we would spend hours on the phone talking and going deeper into our very beautiful connection.

It was confusing for me to share such intimacy and connection so openly and freely, and for Julia to pull away saying she needed to be free. Free from what, I wondered. My projection was that the other guys she previously saw had not shared the same openness, intimacy and connection; surely she wanted freedom from them, not me?

I knew there was something truly amazing about Julia and our connection and the deeper we went into it the more I wanted us to be together. But the more Julia, when we were apart, pulled away. Julia wanted to be free to sleep with other men, which was

46

very hard for me. I had experimented with 'open' relationships before, having lived at various communes in India where this was the norm. I was very aware that for me to be in a relationship like that I had to hold a bit of something back. I was way past this with Julia. We had decided to commit to each other quite early on and so I had already let go of the part of me I needed to protect.

Having spent a few weeks committed to each other, Julia realised this was not what she wanted. What she wanted was to see other guys. There were reasons that she had come to this decision but for me, who had completely let go into being with Julia it was hard. We had continued to go deeper and deeper, time flew, sex was amazing and getting better and better. I didn't want to share Julia with other guys.

Let the process begin

My heart was very heavy and was in pain. The pain grew and I found it so hard to see a way out. I stayed with the intense feelings and they got more intense. I was in love and my lover wanted to see other men. To find myself in a situation of such vulnerability was quite scary. I am not a fearful man, in fact I feed off fear in certain situations, but this was different. This was my heart wide open to this beautiful woman. This was vulnerability in its extreme and diving headlong in was the hardest experience of my life. I had to question my feelings of not being good enough, I had to look at the trust I have in the world: was I really going to be alright and get through this? I also had to look at why I would hide a part of myself or hold back a part of myself in relationships to keep safe. I had taken the plunge and my greatest fears were unfolding. What a great gift – to be able to live your greatest fear while being fully supported in it!

I really did feel fully supported in my heartache and process. No one has ever held me in my pain like Julia did. She has an amazing capacity that allowed me to investigate the darkest, hidden depths of my soul without judgement or agenda. When I was a child growing up there was a lot of pain and heartache and I had learned to cope and manage this for myself, completely unsupported. To now be with the woman I love, investigating my deepest hurt and to be so supported in this was profoundly healing.

My process and heartache went on, and on. It felt like it would never end. At one point Julia was away with a friend and I felt so alone. Communicating with Julia by email had become confusing, with me getting the wrong end of the stick on a few occasions. Misunderstandings led to more confusion and I began to wonder how much more my heart could take. I had experienced big losses as a kid and the pain I was in was bringing all the hurt back up. My feelings of abandonment and being left were brought to the surface and I was able to stay with all the feelings. I made damn sure I didn't create any stories, pass blame, or project anything onto Julia. I knew that for me to have these feelings arise meant they were within me and not because of anything outside of me. In fact, if truth be known, if something outside of me triggers feelings like the ones I was experiencing it was because of what was going on inside of me. I had, at some level, invited it in.

It was time for Julia to run the Brighton Marathon. I had received an email from her that I mis-interpreted, I thought she'd had enough and was off, that was it. It was all over. I spoke to Julia and said I did not want to come to the marathon and the after-party. I could not face meeting her friends having just parted ways. I was still up for hooking up with her though. Julia read into this that I didn't want to come and see her and that it was all over. My heart was in so much pain, I was losing the woman I loved and there was nothing I could do, it seemed. Julia called me back minutes before her next clients arrived and we decided I should drive down to see her, a very good decision as all the mis-understandings were cleared up. We had a great weekend and the after-party was a great success.

Time moved forward and Julia wanted to meet up with Tom, one of her previous lovers, and what's more, a friend of mine. I had come to terms with this happening and realised that it was part of the process. It would be interesting to see, having spent six or so weeks in this deep process how I would feel. I was actually quite okay with Julia meeting Tom.

I gained a lot of freedom – this could have been my worst fear realised, but I was cool. I had freed myself from so much past pain, and felt so much more 'in my body'. The body is such a good barometer of how we feel about things and I was clear, clearer than I had ever been. We met up the following weekend and things between us were brilliant. We had the most amazing weekend full of love and laughter. We parted after that weekend feeling so very close, full of love and intimacy.

Julia phoned me saying Tom wanted to come and see her again. I knew that he wanted to 'get Julia back' and this was an attempt, on some level, to drive us apart. I was distraught. I was just entering a meeting when I heard and was thrown back into my process. Just when you think it is over – whoosh.

Julia met with him and I was very angry. 'How could she do this?' was what I was thinking. We'd had such an amazing weekend together and now she was with someone else. Julia stayed in touch with me throughout my ordeal by text. We spoke late at night and I was still upset. It took a while, but speaking to Julia I realised she loved me and this whole process was about both of our fears: Julia not wanting to commit; and me not wanting to share her – both reasons boiling down to not wanting to be abandoned.

Once again I stayed with the feeling of being completely vulnerable, my heart still aching and full of grief and pain. I could feel things were shifting in me, I was responding to situations in different ways, watching all the time with both surprise and awe. It seemed that feeling these deep wounds and allowing them to breathe was very healing and freeing. They no longer had a hold on me. My responses were no longer guided by my pains and emotional wounds, but still my heart was heavy, the woman I loved was not completely with me as she maintained her need for freedom.

I could see that Julia had been disappointed so many times – why would she trust me not to be as she expected? I could also see that her pattern supported all her adaptations of being wrong. I saw Julia the first time we made love, how amazing and beautiful she really was, of course I could see there was nothing about Julia that was "wrong"!

I completely understood Julia wanting her freedom. She had gone into relationship enthusiastically in the past and been disappointed, and of course was expecting the same this time round. She did not want to risk repeating this pattern. It's easier to be in an open relationship, not having to totally commit to a lover – effectively 'putting all her eggs in one basket'. I understood this, but it wasn't what I wanted! I had met a very special woman in Julia. I could see most of the other men she had been in relationship with had not 'met' her. By this I mean were not dedicated to being conscious, to looking at every reaction or pattern that came up for them, to clearing it, not alone but consciously with one another. It takes a brave soul and Julia was the first person, let alone woman, I had met and felt I could do this with. So here I was with a decision to make: Julia wanted her freedom, I wanted to be in a relationship with her, and I could see we were both on the same path of consciousness.

When we were together it was amazing, whether making love or cooking or running or just chatting – it felt like we were consciousness embodied in human form coming together. My choice was: do I stay and try to work it out, or do I go because this was a hard situation that brought up a lot of my insecurities? Of course I decided to stay. That decision was very empowering for me – this was MY choice. It was hard. The issues that came up for me were all based around feeling abandoned. My parents divorced when I was five years old and I had a great sadness, feeling I had effectively lost my dad. This became a pattern of mine: people that meant a lot to me being torn from my life in situations beyond my control. Because it was my choice to stay, I had put this situation within my control.

My love for Julia gave me the momentum and strength to want to work this old pattern out, and to work it out with another person eager to do so consciously. This became my endeavour, I consciously allowed the powerful emotions and feelings to course through my being, trusting they would clear. And, after ten weeks of intense 'going in' to all the feelings and allowing them to pass, they did – and I wondered what all the fuss was about! It still fascinates me that, having changed MY energy, the whole dynamic changed, eventually leading to Julia committing to being my girlfriend.

A Girlfriend for a Year Diaries: Part Two

On 12 May 2013, at 12:55, Julia wrote:
Hi dearest Tom,
I hope you are having an amazing time in Wales. I love the mountains of
Morocco – I'm here with Anadi and I just wanted to say to you that I have
said to him today that I will commit to him and me for a year exclusively
and see where we are at after that! I wanted to tell you as I am your friend
and ally always.
With love,
J xxx

On 12 May 2013, at 17:12, Tom wrote:
How lovely to hear it – I feel delighted for you both – he's a beautiful man
and beautiful soul as are you – both lovely friends to me and I truly wish you
both the most wonderful time. I can imagine it being hugely good for both of
you in terms of each of your life's work too.
Excellent, excellent – my limitless blessings to both of you xxx

**Day 1: Sunday 12th May. *'He loved me, in a way that I have*
*never been loved before'***

Anadi and I sat on the roof terrace of the Imlil Lodge enjoying
our breakfast, though a little shaky from lack of sleep. We had
talked a lot during the night and slept for just three hours. My
heart had hurt and Anadi had held me. He was clear and still and
he loved me, in a way that I have never been loved before.

We were recovering from our 35 mile 'jaunt' in the Atlas
Mountains. The experience had shown us our unbreakable bond.
Our relationship was transparent in the mountain air, and
through the haze of low blood sugar and high altitude the love

between us had shimmered and led us over the mountains and eventually home.

'What do you want?' I asked him. 'With us, I mean.'

'I want to be with you.'

I listened to this beautiful man, exposed and vulnerable before me, declaring his love for me and saying what he wanted. For months I had been pulling free. I wanted my freedom, I didn't want to be restricted – all things that Anadi felt too. I wanted to sleep with other men, seeing this as a symbol of my freedom, in a way. This was beyond his emotional boundaries, and yet he had stretched and stretched and worked and worked to accommodate this.

I looked at Anadi in front of me, loving him with all my heart, and knew that a decision had to be made. I got up to go to the bathroom and as I went through the door, I thought of something I suggest to my clients – a 'no exit' arrangement for an agreed period of time: a year, that felt good. I returned to Anadi.

'What do you want?' I asked him again.

'I know you want to be free' he replied.

'Tell me what you truly want' I said again.

'I love you and I want to be with you' he replied.

'I'll do this for a year, just you and me.' I said. 'I'll fully commit; I'll be your girlfriend for a year. And then on May 12th next year, we can see where we are.'

We travelled to Marrakech and arrived at a beautiful hotel. It was my birthday, and we shared a love-filled day of being together over breakfast on the terrace, the leafy balcony in the hotel; wandering the streets; eating in a roadside café; being led through the streets by a local guide. He took us to his friend's shop where I bought presents, bright colourful bags, and a magic genie lamp and scarf for me, then back to our hotel for a late afternoon of lovemaking and lying talking in the bath.

We sat, sipping mint tea and eating cake, then drinks on the roof terrace before an evening meal in a restaurant with rose petals on the table. I'd mentioned it was my birthday to the hotel, and for dessert we were served a delicious 'birthday cake' with a candle. I was serenaded by four men, one with a lute, in white robes with red hats on their heads.

Day 2: Monday 13th May. *A letting-go had occurred, no limits now, nowhere we could not go*

On the plane back to the UK with Anadi, I prayed.

'Please show me truth. I don't mind how it comes, lead me wherever I must go, for I am ready. Please guide Anadi and I to the higher purpose of our relating, deeper into our path of love and consciousness, both within our own lives and within our relationship.'

A letting-go had occurred, no limits now, nowhere we could not go. We had achieved the depths and the heights that I always imagined truly possible, as travellers on the path to deeper love, consciousness and growth through intimacy and connection.

Day 3: Tuesday 14th May. *It was a wrench to part and my life felt paler*

Today Anadi and I travelled back from Marrakech and had to say goodbye to one another at the airport. It was a wrench to part and my life felt paler. I missed him straight away. I texted him when I got back, but he didn't reply. This spun me into my old 'stuff', my pain of abandonment, loss and separation, out-dated stuff I had thought - clearly not! I had warned him he would have to work hard and I would be demanding. Although I always take responsibility for my pain, maybe I needed to heal now by being safe, feeling safe; rather than working through the pain of abandonment? I felt that a goodnight text would have held me safe.

Day 4: Wednesday 15th May. *I told some friends about being a girlfriend for a year*

I told some friends about being a girlfriend for a year. They were pleased and happy for me. I also I mentioned to a client that, 'my guy lives in London'. I was telling everyone, in fact, because it felt right, like the safety of surrendering allowed Anadi and I to be together and explore without limits. Despite my reservations, I felt free within the space we had created, that we could both heal and become more whole. But I also felt more vulnerable and slightly mad! I missed Anadi but we had made plans to see each other at the weekend, which excited me. I felt full of love for my crazy, druggy, jailbird boyfriend.

Day 5: Thursday 16th May. *First I knew I had to learn to love myself*

A friend mentioned that Anadi and I had 360 days left of this year as boyfriend and girlfriend. 360 is a complete circle. I missed Anadi, his presence. My body ached for him. My head was full of thoughts and feelings.

I feel at ease.

I love him.

I trust him.

I love telling people about being a girlfriend for a year.

We kept in touch by text and then talked in the evening. As always, a couple of hours passed so easily – and I don't like the phone as a medium to talk! With Anadi I could talk forever, feeling a limitlessness to our dialogue, a conversation that never ended.

He told me that a friend of his had asked about our holiday, and while Anadi was speaking, said:

'You two are going to get married.'

'Where did that come from?' Anadi asked.

'I don't know'.

He spoke to another friend about the mountain adventure:

'I bet you got irritated with one another.'

'No we didn't.'

'You've got a gem there' he said.

Anadi talked of getting a flat near me, and of keeping his flat in London too, so we could spend more time together. He had been telling people that I was the love of his life.

I had supper with Jane and she said that she thought Anadi would be big enough for me, that it had only just begun and that it could be limitless. Again, I was full of thoughts.

I wonder where we will go?

I wonder where we can go?

What is limitless love?

What does it look like?

I had longed for and wanted connection above everything. But first, I had to learn to love myself.

Day 7: Saturday 18th May. *If you can feel it you can heal it*

Anadi and I had amazing sex – twice. He arrived and we talked and talked before going to bed, getting up at midnight to make supper, then back to bed, finally sleeping at 4am. I will never forget the sex we had in the early hours of Sunday morning. Something shifted with the deepening commitment to one another. We were more connected and there was surrender within our lovemaking that I have not experienced before.

Are people afraid of this? These spaces are incredibly vulnerable and if we haven't done the work to connect with ourselves, then letting go could engender a fear of annihilation and of never returning to 'normal' again, a loss of self and an increased fear of loss of the other, to whose love we have entrusted our safekeeping. With Anadi, I experienced there being no veil. We could look into one another's eyes with complete clarity.

We had one conversation in which I felt like 'an impossible woman'. We were planning to go to a friend's birthday party a long drive away, and he had already promised to take another friend. I expressed that I would prefer if it were just us in the car, although of course I would honour his commitment. When he didn't immediately say he would of course prefer to be just with me too, my deep down fear of abandonment and 'not being important' was activated – but not for long. I worked with it and he reassured me.

I was interested that this deep pain could still be accessed. It meant it could be worked on – 'If you can feel it you can heal it' – and in truth I welcomed the opportunity to identify where I was not whole and so seek to heal and grow.

Day 8: Sunday 19th May. *We wrote down our dreams*

We went to sleep at 3am after another night of incredible lovemaking. I wondered if I would still be writing about this much sex at the end of the year – and hoped so! Despite our late night, we woke at 9am and stayed in bed talking and making love until 3pm, when we finally got up and went for 'lunch'. We wrote down our dreams: our individual dreams and our dreams of our life together.

I wrote that I wanted to run and write and grow deeper in relationship with Anadi; that I wanted to be able to do handstands and cartwheels again and be free of any injury and pain in my body; and that I wanted to trust which way my healing

57

gift would take me. Anadi wrote that he wanted to develop his software and create a sustainable and enjoyable business and way of life; to grow deeper in consciousness himself; and grow deeper in relationship with me.

Together we wrote that we would create an abundant life from the energy of our souls, not from our minds; that we would trust which way that led us and enjoy a life of conscious living.

Later we went running on the downs as the light was fading. It was a magical time to be there, with the sea sparkling below us.

Day 10: Tuesday 21st May. *Picking him up on his stuff is difficult as it has not been welcome before*

It was a busy day for me, starting work at 7am with clients from London and finishing at 8.30pm. My day was thankfully broken up by tea with my friend Steph at the Grand Hotel – a grand finale to my birthday celebrations. She told me the pictures of Anadi and I on Facebook made her think we would be announcing we were getting married.

The mountain story, posted on my blog, had already been read by many people. Anadi's Dad had read and commented on it, as had his friend Yogi. It seemed as if everyone had read our story.

I looked forward to hearing Anadi's voice after my mega day. I love talking with Anadi, it is difficult to stop. In fact he had emailed me in the morning to say he found it hard not to be with me. I felt the same. Anadi was open to me noticing every little thing within our relating; something that was good for me, and very new.

I was still a bit uncomfortable with it though. I am happy to always take responsibility for my stuff but picking him up on his stuff was difficult as it had not been welcome before. But he had been open to it, genuinely wanting to learn, particularly when I explained it was the way to really see other people; by seeing everything in ourselves and being honest about it - and trying to do it 24/7.

Day 11: Wednesday 22nd May. *Interdependence and letting go of being independent, he and I in it together*

Anadi said that he would marry me, and that he is really getting what having a relationship is: interdependence and letting go of being independent, he and I in it together. He said I am showing him what true love is and he is happy showing me what true love is. He runs with everything I notice or comment on, and has said he wants to do this with me fully. No one has before. Many have wanted to marry me, but this time feels to be a marriage of souls. It's what I've always dreamed of.

I had an amazing session with Ros, my therapist and supervisor. I wanted to explore my feelings of lack of safety that had arisen since promising to be Anadi's girlfriend for a year. There was a terror of abandonment deep inside me, which could arise simply from the absence of a reply to a text. It was old stuff that I recognised, and had shifted at one level, but which screamed, 'This is not safe – danger, danger!' from deep inside me.

Ros and I explored my history. Of course, I knew the story well, and so did she, having been working with me for more than 20 years. The people I entrusted myself to when I was young, the people I surrendered myself to body and soul, were my mother and my running coach Tim. My mother died when I was 16 years old. She left me in a way, the person who knew me and saw me and understood me inside out was gone. Tim, in effect, abused me and the trust I put in his hands.

It is no wonder that intimacy had not felt safe for me, but I'd still sought deep, connected love all my life. I'd leapt enthusiastically into relationships and marriages, but never really committed to the whole, 'for better and for worse', thing – as Ros said, 'You left when it got worse.' And yet I had always longed and yearned for connection. I had always known that I was capable of a love so deep. (Anadi said to me that, when we are making love, my eyes are so intense that he can see why men who are not honest and clear with themselves would run from the light and the intensity.)

I concluded with Ros that I was not expressing the truth of who I am if I didn't own my longing for a deep, connected, intimate relationship. I had come to the place where staying 'safe' and 'free' had become uncomfortable and ultimately would mean I was 'stuck' and 'trapped' by my own wound. I now saw that in loving Anadi I had the chance to become truly free and to experience relating in the way I had always dreamed.

Day 13: Friday 24th May. *'It's not for a year, is it? It's forever, this'*

I spent the day with men, hearing only one female voice all day. I ran with my friend Jim in the morning, telling him all about Anadi, and the process we had been through with each other and with Tom. He commented that he didn't know how Anadi held on through the process, given that he was really into me. (When I later mentioned this to Anadi, he said that he did it because he was into me.) Jim said I should go away more often, that it accelerated things within me. He was right, the break in Morocco did accelerate things and I came home very shifted and happy to be a girlfriend for a year.

As we spoke on the phone last night Anadi said, 'It's not for a year, is it? It's forever, this.'

60

I left home at 9.40pm, after a day of therapy with men, and arrived after driving through rain and dark to my oasis, Anadi's house, where he was waiting with a meal ready to eat at midnight. We laughed and talked a lot before making love and falling asleep at 4am.

I was getting used to late bedtimes and early mornings. It felt natural to spend time together and not worry about the clock. It seemed that we healed each other by being together, which was like sleeping, in a way. The connection seemed to double and multiply our soul energy, already strong in us as individuals.

Day 14: Saturday 25th May. *We were well received, with many comments about the love that is tangible between us*

We got up and ran two laps of Trent Park, seven miles in total, both feeling amazingly bright on four hours sleep. The trees were lush and green, and there were groups of people running and playing sport. I felt happy and alive.

Later, we drove to the Mind Body Spirit (MBS) show in Olympia. This was our first day 'out' as a couple and we were well received, with many comments about the love that was tangible between us. People said we looked good together and wanted to know how we met. Someone said that a picture on Facebook was 'pure love'. Mel, the director of MBS, said 'You're made for each other'. He also told me to look after Anadi, to help make his businesses successful and that he was a 'good boy'. A friend of Anadi's said that 'love suits him'. Another gave us a price reduction because, 'You're a lovely couple'. Kyle, who wrote *Angel Prayers*, asked me, 'Is he your toy boy?'

'He is' I said.

'You're lucky to have such a spiritual man. Anadi is all heart'.

61

I saw how much people want love, to see it, to be it, to be in it, to feel it, to experience it in their lives: to love and to be loved in return.

Understanding the Process: Staying Safe

When we were little, we were very vulnerable. We needed to be fed and looked after, and we needed to keep safe. We saw the adults around us as the people who could take care of us and look after us.

As children we do not think that the adults don't know what they are doing. We do not know that they are often acting from a wounded place themselves and stuck in habitual patterns and acting out of fear – keeping safe themselves, though usually unconsciously.

People act from within a paradigm (the distinct set of beliefs and ideas that we have formed of the world and our life, made up through the influences in childhood) that is familiar to them; a set of beliefs, ideas and conditioning that they have internalised from their childhood influences. Unless this is challenged and examined, these scripts run on and people often live life by default. This can result in a happy life if it is in alignment with a person's true expression, and it can result in a 'successful life' if people attain levels of success in school, work, choice of partner and how well the children do. But it is often an 'unconscious life'. The deeper stirrings of expression are ignored if they do not seem to fit the paradigm.

To survive as children, if we sensed we were in danger of being 'cast out' through disapproval or abandonment then we would likely adapt our behaviour to make sure that we remained safe. Alternatively, we might 'act out' because of the restrictions or circumstances of our upbringing.

As children, we adapted and survived – which demonstrates our amazing capacity – and life took on a rhythm, and unfolded. Many live their lives out without ever questioning their beliefs or their actions. They might look at others who are different with surprise and confusion, but it may not open the door to exploration.

People often stay safe because:
• They do not know there is a different way
• They do not know that they have the power within themselves to make changes
• Even if they do know; making changes challenges their current situation too much and they are more comfortable with what they know
• Fear limits people; not knowing what is beyond the leap into the new is overwhelming
• People keep re-creating the same patterns and distract themselves with dramas and habitual conversations and habits that keep them locked in and time passes.

A Process and To Process

A process is when you recognise that there is a disturbance within. You are emotionally upset by something, there is a difficulty in a relationship, you are having difficulty achieving a goal: 'I am going through a process'.

To process is when, having recognised the disturbance, instead of making a 'drama' about what is going on, or about the other people concerned, you reflect. You turn a process, which in some way arises beyond your control, and you take control of it by 'processing' it, turning the noun into the verb. Once you have acknowledged you are in a process, you can start processing.

If you are upset then something from the past has been touched, which alerts you to the fact that work needs to be done. To process you must focus on what is coming up for you and not the other people involved in the present situation. You must take responsibility for your own projections onto the situation.

Clearing the Blockage

Clearing refers to clearing the stuff that arises because of this situation. This entails recognising the wound that has been touched, what you are seeing through the filter of your pain, and then working to go into the pain; to access what has been touched, to recognise that you are now in the past, and to seek to heal the pain.

It can also entail seeing aspects of your lost or hidden or disowned self in front of you in the situation. When we react to people in a deep way it is often because they are displaying an aspect of ourselves that we are not living out. If we are distressed by someone's loud voice and speaking about themselves, this can point to the place we have been silenced and want to learn to speak our truth. So, recognising a process and then processing is about reclaiming our lost selves. It is about healing our wounds and becoming whole again.

This can take many forms. Some people find talking therapies useful. Others use writing as a way of healing. Some draw strength from mindfulness, meditation or physically processing their emotions, for example, through running, as I do. Everyone is different and there is no 'right' way to process and clear: the important thing is that you allow yourself to clear rather than reacting from your 'wounded' place and turning your process into your partner's problem.

Going Through the Process

Anadi and I both went through our own process as our relationship evolved. I was drawn to face my emotions and reactions surrounding abandonment, feeling free and commitment. And he had his own experiences to process and reactions to work through.

When he said that he was really getting what having a relationship is: interdependence and letting go of being independent, he and I in it together, he was showed his commitment to going through a process – and sharing his own process with me.

In turn, this commitment helped reassure me about my own process – and reminded me that he was happy following a path that had previously been denied by previous partners. Of course, the process is on-going. I still had my own process to follow – in accepting that I could 'pick him up on his own stuff' when it had not been welcome before.

A Girlfriend for a Year Diaries: Part Three

Day 18: Wednesday 29th May. *I had the time and like all journeys, I eventually reached my destination*

After a tiring drive on the M25, I arrived in St Albans. I'd stopped off en-route to do some healing with a friend who was bed-ridden and dropped in on my auntie Helen – also bed-ridden. The drive had been no more challenging than I imagine regular M25 drivers find all the time: a journey that my sat-nav said would take 54 minutes took, in the end, two and a half hours. But I chatted to Anadi who was driving the other way to junction 22, listened to Alan Watts talking about Zen (which helps when stuck in traffic!) and generally appreciated that everyone around me was experiencing the same thing.

It may have taken longer than I'd planned, but I had the time and, like all journeys, I eventually reached my destination. Anadi was waiting for me in the road, which made finding my destination nice and easy. We had a coffee, then went to the radio station, where I was heading to be part of a show.

It was fun. The presenter, Liz, asked me about conscious relationship. I started by telling her how important it was to have a relationship with yourself.

'How can you have a relationship with yourself?' she asked me. 'How does one get to allow themselves that opportunity if they're already in a relationship? What if you're like me and when you're in a relationship you're so consumed with that relationship you almost forget yourself? Is that not the difference between a conscious relationship and the relationship that most people have?'

'I don't think it's about not being in a relationship'. I replied. 'I think, actually, we learn to have our relationship with ourselves in relationship, because we're always in relationship with everybody we meet. Being conscious is about recognising that who we are is going to have come from all those influences. Being in relationship with yourself is about starting to get to know how you respond in any given moment. It's about deciding that you want to take notice.'

Liz went on to ask about more about romantic relationships.

'I know so many women in their fifties who have been married and are now divorced and may have short-term relationships, but actually have found a much more fulfilling relationship with themselves. I certainly have, and I feel at the moment that would be obstructed by someone else coming in.'

'It might mean that the relationship would bring up again the unresolved places within you'. I replied.

'So you need to go there?'

'It is always our choice ultimately, and there are many ways of relating. But what happens when people are unconscious in relationship, in any relationship intimate or otherwise, and likely all of us have been unconscious at some time, is that we don't realise what's happening. Most of relationship is driven by our unconscious. We are attracted unconsciously by people with both positive and negative characteristics of our caretakers, and our inner child wants to get its needs met. We will gravitate towards people who it thinks will lead to us getting those needs met this time. What tends to happen is that the negative characteristics cause problems. The romantic phase is wonderful, because there's a recognition. Our partner will carry parts of our disowned, lost, hidden self. You meet a person with a complementary lost self, maybe someone who was told to be quiet when they were little, and they became quiet. You were told to be quiet, and perhaps you adapted by becoming very chatty. Then over time, that very thing that attracted you, comes to piss you off. You wish they would speak, because they never speak, and they wish you would shut up, because you never shut up! Then the power struggle begins, if you've gone in unconsciously.'

'That sounds like me in my last relationship!' said Liz. 'My partner said the things he loved about me at the start are now the things he hates about me. He actually said that!'

The first hour of the show was spent exploring and explaining – which led Liz to say she'd like a session: therapy on air! So for the second half of the show, I worked with her. We only had forty minutes, so I just worked with her as best I could and responded as I would in my room – a new challenge. I was slightly aware of Anadi and the producer there, and I was shaking in the news and music breaks, but essentially I just did as I always do with clients: I asked to be what she needed.

I have always trusted that I won't 'get in the way' of my healing gift. It is the same in running: if I 'surrender my acts to the divine' nothing ever goes 'wrong', but if I 'get in the way' and allow my mind to get involved, all manner of havoc can ensue. And so with my work with people. The sentence, 'Please help me be what they need' has allowed me to trust that my wisdom and healing will flow and that I don't need to use my mind first. I use my heart and intuition as guides and let the mind follow with the ideas, the learning, the education – all I have to offer.

I couldn't face driving again afterwards and I wanted to be with Anadi, I hadn't really seen him. So I followed him home where we ate, talked and made love. At 5am my alarm got me up and I drove home in the pouring rain after four hours sleep.

Day 20: Friday 31st May. *It was nearly light, but it seems I'm getting used to it*

Anadi arrived as I finished work and we decided to go for cocktails. We left at 9.45pm and were amazed to find it was 12.45am when we returned home. How did a quick drink before

69

supper turn into three hours? Not for the first time, I found myself thinking that time seemed to do strange things when we were together.

I made us a very late supper. How I did it, I don't know as I was feeling properly drunk after just two margaritas. We had great sex – though I can't remember it that well, due to the cocktails. Another 3.30am bedtime, it was nearly light, but it seemed I was getting used to it!

Day 21: Saturday 1st June. *I talked about it and said sorry, but somehow it spiralled out of control*

A conversation with Anadi set off my reactivity and I felt the best way to clear it was to separate myself and write down my feelings as honestly as I could. We were looking at holidays which Amy had planned for us. Anadi wanted to check out flights and I knew Amy had checked everything.

I reacted. It irritated me that he wanted to check. Then I felt guilty for the reaction and so I talked about it and said sorry, but somehow it spiralled out of control. This can happen all too easily when we are reacting from our past wounds and not the present situation. I turned to free writing, 'in my wound and from my wound', letting the words flow to help me process my emotions. I have included it here, unedited, to show the authentic flow and process.

The Wounded Self in Dialogue

I am still upset and I can't get back. We talked it all through and it was fine in a way, but it feels too hard that no one seems to have my capacity to stay with pain without getting tired and I feel disappointed and sad and very lonely.

I imagine he doesn't feel great, but I want to be alone to regroup and to gather myself back, instead of being in this mire of emotion and pain and a real feeling of abandonment. I want the safety back, and the ease. This is why I don't like relationships, I don't like the separation that seems almost inevitable, particularly with me. I am too much, too intense and I can sustain and maintain and stay engaged long after others just get tired and give up and lie down and sleep.

I hate it, and however unreasonable it seems I just hate it. I'm never sure it's worth being in a relationship for the upside when the down for me is so miserable and I'd rather be alone than experience this pain. I feel lost – like now this has happened there is no return, the good bit is over and now we will have this periodically and then I'll decide to end it because I'll get disappointed and lonely and he will always lie down and I'll get impossible and push it to the end. Then I'll feel better again and be free to be me and not feel bad about myself.

I feel bad now because it's me, it's always me. I always ruin it because I want too much and I need too much and I am too much in pain and so the talking stops. It's fine if it's light and loving and yet when he was in pain I didn't lie down, I didn't get tired and look pale and stop talking. But of course it was me who created that so it's me who is bad and wrong and spoils everything and then people die and I am alone.

How I wish someone would stay with this, this is the bit I want held, the rest is easy. I am amazing, so of course it's easy to talk all night and be open and loving and free but this is the part that is hurt and needs loving. But, as I know and have always known, no one can love this part that I don't love myself, no one will stay with this part I reject in myself – why would they? If I don't love me then they'll leave too.

So the truth is it's up to me and then it's all fine. But boy am I angry and sad and alone and I want the weekend to end so I am then free again to be me and feel okay and see myself reflected back in strength and ease, rather than this disease deep and dark in me and now he has gone. They all go, they all leave, the moment this shows. This is the reason my relationships end; this is the reason.

This is the reason I wanted him to stay, this is the point I wanted him to never leave, to stay and see it through until he knew I was okay. But of course I'm the wrong one so he doesn't have to stay, but when he was vulnerable I stayed. But then I was wrong then, I'm always wrong. I don't want this if he can't stay with this. It's always the same. I have more capacity than anyone I know. I am so angry, so sad, so alone.

I went into the bedroom after writing and said how I felt: angry, and upset. Anadi was amazing. He came and hugged me and we talked and talked. After some time, I felt another shift and a layer of pain leave. We then had amazing 'altered state' sex, and fell to sleep at our usual time of 3.30am.

Day 23: Mon 3rd June. *We slept in each other's arms, and parted with heavy hearts*

Anadi and I decided that we don't want to be parted, and decided to live together from July. My home could become our home and I could keep working there: together all the time. It was going to happen. I wondered what would happen to our sleep patterns then. I wondered what would happen, full stop!

It felt good, that this was the way we must go to allow the motion of the energy that was propelling us together – and out into the world too, it seemed. The more we cleared our stuff together, the more altered states we were experiencing, and the more our deepest qualities came to the fore.

This feeling of an altered state experience had happened a lot since Anadi and I got together. It felt a bit like having had a cocktail: slightly surreal, spaced out, looking in on the world like it was a film – to an even greater extent than I usually did! It was a very free feeling, like nothing mattered. I felt quite disconnected to my body and mind, like I was floating and could step out of my body should I want to. Anadi said he thinks this happens because we are both so committed to clearing and releasing all the rubbish within us, that this makes our energy fields different. Also, being with each other a lot meant we were not attached to the limited thought patterns that often keep people stuck and in fear.

Yesterday we woke at 9.40 and had quite a hurried time to get to the Western Lawns to see my friend Kev at the end of his bike race. He finished 3rd, after a strong ride. Anadi and I chatted a bit to him and to his wife, Brioni, and then headed off to the hills to run. We ran into the Hollow and up the side of Beachy Head – a steep climb!

Again, time seemed to slip away when we were together: by the time we'd shared a bath and eaten 'brunch', it was about 4pm.

Between then and 1am was a blur. We made the first in our series of educational videos, but I finished it in an altered state so had no idea what I'd said. We chatted a lot, I know, ate more food and created our intro, then recorded the first one of the series. I felt clearer, more open and 'shifted' since the 'demons' from the past arose and were released yesterday. We slept in each other's arms, and parted with heavy hearts.

Understanding the Process:
The Smallest Things and
The Stories We Tell Ourselves

Writing now, with my awareness of my wound, I can see that when Anadi and I were planning our holiday and he wanted to check the flights, it alerted me to an old pattern I had known before, of being with men who needed to be 'in control of everything'. At the deepest level, it reminded me of being with my Dad who wanted to control me and everything, or at least it seemed that way from my perspective.

As we all know, the most blazing arguments are often about 'nothing'. The smallest thing in the present can activate a deep wound from the past. And so we react with strong emotion to something that seems small to the other, or we withdraw, because the 'danger' of staying open seems too great.

For me, one of the 'smallest things' is 'the T word' – tired. I have found that in every relationship I have been in, the man talks about being tired a lot. I have an issue with this, as I see tiredness as an exit (which it often is). I am better with tiredness in Anadi now, as he doesn't disconnect when tired, but it is still an adaptation of mine to never let on if I am tired.

Repeating the Story

My own contribution to the dynamic that led to the end of my previous relationships was that, in the beginning, I would act in the way I did with my Dad to ensure 'connection' – which in truth disconnected me, because it was about accommodating someone else's needs. Then, at the first hint of 'control', I would react, often unreasonably, as in this case, projecting that the person was trying to take over. In some cases this was true as I had chosen controlling men; but with Anadi it wasn't: it was a clear case of him being curious about the flights that were being chosen.

My reaction was to the past. I projected my childhood and previous relationships onto the situation. From there, the pattern I played out historically was to feel 'bad' and 'wrong' about my behaviour, and I would leave, having created my 'way out' so that I wouldn't have to feel the pain of self-hatred.

Changing the Story

In this relationship I was learning to stay. I was the one that needed to stay, not Anadi. It was me who played that part of our dynamic out, but it meant we both experienced the lack of safety around our childhoods, brought into our present relationship, and had our fears confirmed that being in a relationship was not a safe thing.

Understanding your own, 'smallest things' can be a key to unlock functional – even thriving – relationship. The techniques explained in *Understanding the Process: Staying Safe* can help you reach this point. You may also find it useful to take an honest look at previous relationships. Are there any patterns that have played out again and again. Are there any times you can think of where you used, 'You always...' or 'You never...' to confront a partner about things that you felt were issues? These phrases can often indicate where you may find your 'smallest things': they often say more about the person 'blaming' than the person 'being blamed'. And of course, the same is true if you've been on the receiving end of, 'You always,' and 'You never'.

In the aftermath of a relationship, it can be all too easy to accept any blame or try to 'forget about it' in an effort to move on. However, analysing and identifying your own patterns can make it much easier to avoid making the same mistakes again. It can help you understand the stories that you have internalised: which may be true but can also be our own unique fictions – even if they feel as real as reality, if not more so.

Stories as Barriers

As humans, we create stories to make sense of our world. In relationships it is not uncommon for people to weave narratives that unconsciously keep a protective barrier around their wound and support the status quo. This may become very uncomfortable at a level, because it means we do not experience the connection and love we crave; but it seems to protect from hurt.

'Stories' do not need to have complex narratives. They can be as simple as:

'I am set in my ways.'

'I like my life as it is.'

'I am not ready to share my life.'

'I want to have a relationship with myself first'.

But of course, as I told Liz in our interview, we are always in relationship to some extent. We cannot *not* relate. As such, it is worth investigating the stories we tell ourselves, and consider whether they support the protection of a wound – and thus create a place which stops us from going deeper in relating.

Be True to Yourself

Though it may sound complex, really, it's about being truthful with yourself. Honestly reflect on your adaptations. Does your energy feel joyous and alive and connected? Are you still playful and passionate and creative, or is that something you have lost over the course of your life experience and the stories you have internalised? Do you feel weighed down with disappointments and exhausted with years of struggle? If so, you may find yourself freed by letting go of stories that no longer serve you.

We exist in relationship, but it is often hard for people. Sometimes intimacy becomes a cycle of disappointment, and so people create a life without it and feel far happier. If this is the case, it is worth considering whether being alone is a true choice to connect more with yourself and discover who you truly are, or if it's an avoidance of relationship and intimacy? There is nothing wrong with spending time alone – but make sure it is truly a free and honest choice.

The key is to recognise that we all want to connect on some level. This is much easier to do if we teach ourselves to notice where we are disconnected with ourselves and understand the ways in which we can tend to exit from relationship. We need to be present, rather than letting our past dictate our future: be 'here', not 'there'.

To 'be here' requires that we ignore the memories from past hurts and frustrations and limitations so that we are not projecting our past experiences onto what is occurring now. The first step is to explore our paradigm – this means looking closely at where we got our beliefs from, questioning why they resonate for us, examining the stories we tell about ourselves and about life.

If we truly clear the hurt that has arisen from our experiences in the past, to help us be right here, right now, then there is limitless possibility.

A Girlfriend for a Year Diaries: Part Four

Day 24: Tuesday 4th June. *We talk every night and have to stop ourselves from continuing to talk all night*

I went running with Rob, who talked about his friend Caroline's wedding next year.

'You may have two,' I said.

'I was thinking that this morning' he replied. 'After being a girlfriend for a year, what comes next?'

The night before, Anadi and I had talked about one of my main childhood wounds: my wound of abandonment. I managed to talk it through with him in a way I had never have been able to before. He listened to me and 'got it'. He didn't try to rescue and yet this very act healed me profoundly.

Identifying and confronting my own stories has been a long journey for me. Every time I have been in a love relationship, I have found this wound very debilitating. It has meant that I have eventually come to leave the relationship through my fears being realised, though of course this was in large part due to me creating that story and outcome.

The first video that Anadi and I made, on healing wounds, went live today. It covered exactly this - healing my own wounds from the past and using the experience to help others do the same - and was warmly received.

Anadi and I talked for two hours on the phone in the evening. Much as I find that we 'lose time' when we are together, I couldn't say what we talked about, but we talk every night and have to stop ourselves from continuing to talk *all* night.

Day 26: Thursday 6th June. *'The very essence of me is to be free as a bird'*

I woke up with the thought, 'Whatever has possessed me to be talking about houses and living together when the very essence of me is to be free as a bird?'

I don't want to own anything and I want to be free. These are two major principles that have emerged as I have found myself over the past few years. So why was I slipping back into my old pattern of going with what the man wants? I knew I had to email Anadi. I have left the message unedited to show what I shared in full.

Hello my wonderful Anadi!

I have woken up this morning feeling more connected to things being fun and free! And you and I being free to have fun and be together and be creative. I'd like to just write my thoughts if it's OK — doesn't mean they are set in stone of course! :)

Over the past few years I have established that I was much more unhappy owning property and living with a man and doing what he wanted — even though I went along with it, so it looked like I wanted it too. I really don't want to do that all over again and then to feel trapped and heavy and weighed down by earthly things and a 'normal' way of living! I am so totally loving being with you and what we are doing together.

It is evident we both have big commitments work-wise — and even though you say you don't want to do it, you clearly have commitment to it. As do I to my work, and I do want to do it, as it is my path on this planet, I think. Maybe another will emerge, but it seems that I am able to free people and help them to wake up! So on I will go…

This morning when I woke up I was asking myself why I would change what I have deeply come to know: that I don't want to own property, that I would prefer to spend my money travelling about and having fun. That I want to be fully with you when I am with you. That I hate domesticity and all that comes with living with someone — the normal-ness of it — the lack of space to be myself. I hate all that if truth be told – and I've done my research, 25 years' worth of living with other people to establish that I don't want to do it! :)

This is the conclusion I came to – and I think it's the truth of who I am – and maybe you too? We don't know of course, but I don't want the feeling I've had in every single relationship with a man of having to consider them, having to get back home to them, feeling stressed about my work around them.

What I have with you is what I dreamed – a man who is a kindred spirit on the path to consciousness and love, and the way I want to be living, am living – light. This is what I have worked to establish.

I am keen not to repeat patterns. All my life, since Tim, I have joined in a man's dream, thinking it's mine when it wasn't.

I don't want to own any property – I know that deeply.

I want to be free – I know that deeply.

I love my work and all I have created.

I love my running and its importance in my expression.

And – most importantly, the most important thing to me now – is that I love you and I want to keep going deeper and having our relating and love central to all I do.

I do realise that you might have totally different ways of wanting to do this – so we can talk and explore and make lots of love and all will be wonderful, I know that.

I love you so deeply my Anadi.

Julia xxxxx

Day 27: Friday 7th June. *We are 'finding our feet' in all of this and working out what works for 'us'*

Today, I flew to Edinburgh to visit my brother and sister-in-law Sue. I spoke to Anadi all the way to Gatwick, though all I remember is that we briefly covered the fact that I have backed out of living together. Although Anadi was looking forward to

80

being with me more, and felt disappointed, he was totally understanding and said that he didn't want to put us under pressure and trusted it would all unfold. He replied to my email, sharing his thoughts and feelings. I have again, left the message unedited.

Good morning Beautiful,

Thank you for your lovely email. I completely understand where you are coming from with what you say about owning property and living together. My focus with us is to continue deepening our connection and being more and more in love, I am so very happy with that ;-)

I certainly do not want to create any pressure or stress for either of us and the space we create together. I completely 'get' the need to feel free – I have fought for this my whole life. I don't want you or I feeling like we 'have to do' or 'have to be' because of the other.

It was funny getting your text yesterday right as I went into a meeting, again! ;-) Well done you, I had to do a little work to let it all pass and be present.

I was looking forward to spending more time with you, it is such a wrench saying goodbye and parting. I absolutely LOVE waking up with you in the morning, I LOVE seeing your beautiful smile and so both of us moving into the flat felt like a great move. BUT, I do understand all your points and I also would prefer to be in a better financial position before making such a commitment. Although I think you are right in what you say, I did feel a bit upset; I had got my hopes up and thought I would be spending more time with you. It is all good though, gorgeous. I feel like we are 'finding our feet' in all of this and working out what works for 'us'.

Day 28: Friday 8th June. *Being here now is all that is required*

Today was a glorious summer's day in Edinburgh, with bright blue skies and enough glorious sunshine to allow me to have lunch outside, it was heaven. I slept a lot, which I probably needed – nearly eight hours last night and an hour and a half on the sofa this afternoon. I missed Anadi but I felt happy where I was.

I found myself thinking that this year had been the busiest year of my life but I seemed to have the capacity for everything that was asked of me. I felt there was a guiding light, a path, and it was unfolding before me. Maybe all I needed to do was let go? I could feel part of myself trying to direct and maybe I had moved beyond directing the course of my life? Maybe now it was time to allow another level of 'letting go' occur and just see what magic occurred? A mantra came to my mind: Being here now is all that is required.

Before I left for dinner with my brother and his wife, Anadi and I spoke for an hour, which passed in a flash of light, as it always does. He said we had just begun on this journey of love together; I hoped he was right.

What would fully surrendering look like, I wondered? I imagined it would be a feeling rather than a look – and an inner process rather than an outer one –·and then the outer would reflect that process for sure?

Day 29: Sunday 9th June. *It was more the potential I was in love with than the actual relating*

I found myself missing Tom a bit, though not in a big way, as I realised it was more the potential I was in love with than the actual relating. But the connection was real – is real? I knew that I didn't actually want to see him, but perhaps I was just sad about the potential that never was realised.

Day 31: Tuesday 11th June. *I had a sense of what I dreamed being possible*

Last night I stayed with Anadi; which meant a very early start today. I arrived there on Sunday night from Edinburgh. For the first time ever, the plane was on time. I landed, was straight off, found my car and arrived at Anadi's front door soon after.

I had a sense of what I dreamed being possible. I have always dreamed that two people could experience deeper and deeper levels of union and communion, and that relationship could and even should be the place of personal development. With Anadi I was experiencing this.

I had learned that if my being trusted it, my body trusted it. I was instantly 'ready for sex' just speaking to Anadi, hugging him, being near him, so my body certainly knew! It was my intellect that held back a little; the left brain filled with fear, remembering past disappointments when the promise of love came to nothing, and disappointment set in - to be followed by an inevitable ending. I experienced the pain of separation and lost love again and again, and I grieved my mother and my absent father repeatedly in my relationships with men.

Making love together has changed again, as the trust builds. Anadi says that he wishes he could show me my eyes, which are apparently like headlights! We made love, ate food, made love again and slept all night in one another's arms.

This morning, Anadi was willing to go running but reluctant to get out of bed. We managed to get to the park for midday. I realised that I was a changed person, living two lives: my early morning one which existed in the week and meant I could fit running and work in, connect with my friends, and keep a training program going, which would be far harder without my 'running buddies'; and my second life, a life with Anadi, as his lover, with the hope of experiencing a shared future with him: a life that existed until late into the night.

We ran so well, doing a session of two minutes fast, one minute easy, and Anadi went around the park faster than he had ever gone before We then spent the day chatting and eating before making our video about Tantra. I loved creating with Anadi, it flowed.

Our video inspired an email from one of my clients:

I have just watched your brilliant discussion on 'tantra', once again it is so very interesting. There are so many questions that pop up in my head as I listen to you both and then you seem to answer them a few seconds later. The reactivity is a really very hard process to be conscious of 24/7. I am doing my very best, I seem to have very strong reactions to disloyalty or my idea of disloyalty and people that are nasty to me, or again what I perceive as nasty. This is where I need to come back to self to be able to let it go and not react... So much to think about. I think you and Anadi are a great pairing. I am so happy for you both.

I think I may buy a Tantric book after hearing you both talk.

Knowing that Anadi and I were making a connection with people outside our relationship filled me with joy.

Day 33: Thursday 13th June. *Always stay with the connection to self and the relationships*

Anadi sent me an email, in response to me saying to him that if we could be 100% conscious, we wouldn't get drained or tired. We would be able to remember our connection to the divine at all times and so remember and experience our innate power and innocence. Again, I have not edited his words.

My dearest darling Julia, I so love YOU and I LOVE talking with you. I LOVE what we are creating and I truly feel like I have found a fellow spiritual warrior to journey the path with. I love you with all my heart.

I was thinking about the meeting I had yesterday and I was thinking 'If I were Osho' how it would be. I realise if I were an enlightened master I would probably have not felt 'drained', being conscious in this very moment means there is no drain on our energy! I can honestly say there was not a moment I was not conscious, that is my nature, BUT I can see that my expectations of an outcome, my seeing the end result and having to wait for others to go through a process to get to the same conclusion and my wanting this to be successful are what drains me. I think you are right when you said to relax, stay in the moment and always stay with the connection to self and the relationships, then magic happens and the 'right' outcome will occur! That is great, I can chill and enjoy the ride! So thank you gorgeous for your words of wisdom.

Reading his words made me appreciate his commitment to our shared journey – in itself, helping heal some of my childhood 'wounds'.

Day 34: Friday 14th June *Tonight, it all felt a bit much*

Today, I felt stretched so far with non-stop life; it felt like it had been like this for the whole of the year. I had started to forget what it feels like to have days to myself, or even an afternoon or morning. I put it down to being a girlfriend for all of this year – I hadn't committed to being a proper girlfriend until 34 days ago, but I had been one in nature before that, if not in name.

Tonight, it all felt a bit much. I heard the disappointment in Anadi's voice when I said I was working on Sunday afternoon but reassured myself that he tended to be great about my work. I told him tonight that, when we talk, I wait until he relaxes until I can feel connected. He said he'd like to be more aware of that, and I found myself exploring my process.

When Anadi – or anyone – isn't relaxed, I notice it, and don't feel as connected to the person; who in turn is not as connected to themselves as they would be if they were relaxed. I don't think many people truly watch themselves, not truly every breath, every bit of tension.

Anadi said my gift of seeing people is a gift that I was born with, and I agreed. The truth is that I see and hear more than others, which makes my relating quite hard, but also makes it brilliant, because I can connect in a millisecond with anyone I meet as I see them straight away. However, it makes my deep relating a bit hard because the bits in another person that are tense or disconnected are inevitably not available to me – it is like a small shadow going across the face of the person and they are hidden. Although I see and feel the tension and I can still see them, they stop the connecting. I don't mind this at all now – except in Anadi.

This showed me the part of me that longed for connection, longed for what I know is possible in human form. It left me slightly sad to experience the disconnection. It was so minor and it only ever happened at the beginning of a phone conversation. Anadi wanted to know about it – and so I told him – but it felt a bit uncomfortable, as if I was criticising him. Perhaps that is because it came from disappointment and need, so inevitably there was a shard of criticism in there?

I have always believed that love could dive deep and create anything at all on the planet. Loving another human being is all that is important really and if loving another takes us closer to loving ourselves then that is the truth of life, death and love, which are all in the same flow.

Being brave enough to fully love means being brave enough to fully surrender. I knew I had not done that yet. I felt too practical now to fully surrender and yet in the past I had always followed my heart and it had given me the most amazing experiences and taught me more about life than anything I could ever know.

Day 37: Monday 17th June. *I knew he really and truly was going to do this journey with me*

I drove up to London this weekend; a long journey, three hours with lots of traffic and delays. When I arrived we had to go straight out again to get to a concert and so I had the quickest of showers and off we went to catch the train. I had clients to contact, though in retrospect I shouldn't have. Really I wanted to just relax and connect with Anadi, but I played my part in this not happening as I had texts and emails to attend to. So instead of connecting in with him on the train, which would have been the best thing, I answered messages from my clients. This meant that the tiredness I had been feeling did not have the chance to ease away in the space between us.

The concert was awesome, especially Mannose, who showed total connection to the source through his flute playing and his voice. When he sang it was like a direct link to consciousness and all that is powerful and pure. I wanted him to sing some more, though I accessed the disconnection in myself through my tiredness and feeling that Anadi and I hadn't had time together. The music and the chanting reached a place of sadness within me.

After half the concert was done, there was part of Anadi and I that wanted to leave to be together. But it seemed rude on one level, and on another we wanted to experience the whole offering from the performers, Deva and Miten.

The second half was beautiful. They engaged us, the audience, in their chanting and I started to sing along and enjoy the vibration moving through my body. Mannose sung again too, which was worth every second of staying, and played his flute in a way that felt an extension of him and all that he is and all that is in the universe. It truly felt like that, to listen to him and bask in his sound.

We left the building at 11pm, were home by midnight and making love until the early hours, at last connecting fully. I had spoken to Anadi about the feelings of tension within my body, sadness and exhaustion. As we lay together after eating our meal, they melted away through his compassionate listening and melted further under his touch and his embrace.

The next day we drove to Trent Park on a sunnyish June morning. We ran three laps, then drove home and sat in the car chatting, mirroring what my mother and I used to do: just sitting in the driveway in the car, chatting, connected and at ease. I loved it as a child and loved it with Anadi: shared sacred space, nothing to disturb, just 'hands-free' time, all alone, sharing and relaxed. Anadi made us an omelette for our brunch and we passed the rest of the day lying about and chatting.

Night-time came and there was a glitch in communicating. I became uncomfortable pointing out any little bit of disconnection in Anadi – but disconnection is what makes me feel imprisoned in a relationship: those little bits of 'stuff' within a person that, if it is a person I am working with, I am invited to observe.

Within my own relationships historically, even though guys have initially said, 'Yes, how brilliant,' about consciously relating, as the relationship has progressed, I have had to shut gates down to accommodate. Then my soul has started to die and in the end I have had to leave or stay and suffocate.

I realised today that there had been a part of me waiting for this emotional withdrawal. I addressed things with Anadi in bed, which felt uncomfortable, and he went quiet. I kept saying 'speak to me'. He was struggling not to feel criticised and I was struggling to express. I felt bad about myself, and the part that was disappointed to feel the lack of connection was, ultimately, slightly critical through need. The clarity was fully there - and

88

then I ended up crashing about clumsily trying to connect, being 'dramatic'.

I told Anadi that the previous year had been the happiest of my life because I felt so free to be fully me in every area. Well, that was true, but this year had already been richer and deeper and I had grown so much more. I was in love and loved in return. But, not surprisingly, it hurt Anadi and we were both quiet until he said: 'We can't go to sleep like this, beautiful'. I turned towards him and we made love, passionately and completely and fell asleep in each other's arms.

In the morning we spoke truthfully to each other about our own struggles, about what we truly wanted in life. We reiterated that, at the core level, we both wanted consciousness.

Later, I texted Anadi explaining that the reason I don't like relationships is that, though I am free to be connected and use my 'seeing' skills in my work and in my running, it often doesn't feel that way in relationships. He texted back, 'I understand that. I want to be the guy who does that in relationship...' which left me feeling pleasantly stunned.

After Anadi had finished work I called him and I pointed out exactly where he disconnects in dialogue, as a way to protect the other but also to protect himself, and how it disconnects us. He got it. He saw it. He changed it that minute and he genuinely saw that I am seeing and want to share not criticise,. I felt uplifted and free as I knew he really and truly was going to do this journey with me.

Understanding the Process: Reactivity, Disconnection and 'Doing the Inner Work'

No matter how committed you are to relating consciously, in relationship you are still likely to have moments that 'flare up'. Reactivity is always dramatic, as the pain feels authentically painful. A small thing can occur. Maybe someone takes the last egg in the fridge when, 'you knew I was only eating eggs for breakfast'. A big drama can ensue over the last egg being eaten, when in fact the wound triggered is one of not being important or properly considered.

The wounded person feels 'wronged' and so a great drama can ensue, particularly if it touches the wound in the other person of being 'wrong' or 'criticised' - as Anadi and I found.

People can, in the moment, say lots and lots which is not really related to the egg incident at all, and the episode takes on a dramatic quality, the energy and tone of the incident becoming far out of proportion to the actual fact of somebody eating the last egg that was in the fridge.

Understanding Adaptations

Anadi had adapted by processing pain by himself, alone. He found Ecstasy helped him with this, and meditation as well. It worked for him and he became clear, but the very thing that helped him and his adaptation when he was in pain was the very thing that meant he disconnected from me rather than share what was occurring.

The more we related, the more we understood each other's wounds and adaptations. My dad would withdraw, Anadi's dad would shout. If Anadi withdrew, my inner child would feel 'danger', from patterns picked up in my childhood. If I then pushed for connection emphatically, Anadi's own inner child would feel danger. We worked this loop out, and although we occasionally fell back into it, we also saw it and felt it and so saw the loop/conflict as an opportunity for healing.

Disconnection

Most people disconnect rather than go into their wounds. Disconnection can occur in many ways, but essentially it is about not being present with the person you are with. It is about not listening and it is about not sharing what is truthfully going on.

People disconnect in many ways:
By stopping listening
By criticising
By being reactive
By not maintaining eye contact
By stonewalling what has been said
By not owning what the person sees
By replying 'nothing' when asked if there is something going on
By distracting behaviour

In Anadi's case, when he felt something he didn't share it, instead going into his old adaptation of withdrawing to 'sort it out' alone.

Although I've said it before, it is worth repeating: it is important to listen to the body and to fully recognise that 'if you feel it you can heal it'.

Doing the Inner Work

If we want to live a truly conscious life then it is necessary to do the inner work. Not everyone wants this. Often people are at ease with the way they are, so are not motivated to search within. It is not for us to judge or give uninvited advice: everyone has to find their own path.

Socrates has been credited with saying that 'the unexamined life is not worth living', which seems a little extreme to me. As humans we have the capacity to explore and to 'go within'. If we choose not to do this, then it might be that life will be less rich; but on the other hand, inner work often brings on change in our relationships, our way of life and how we make use of our time.

As you know, we all carry wounds from our past and we all adapt to living in a way that protects us. If we choose not to do any inner work, then we might stay stuck within patterns and scripts that keep us in familiar landscape. However, inner work can also be challenging. We do it by noticing if there is anything in our life that we are unhappy with.

Are we repeating any destructive behaviours or patterns?
Is there something we would like that is eluding us?
Do we feel distressed, depressed, unhappy?
Do we lack self confidence and self esteem?
Do we have difficulty in relationships?
Do we have difficulty with eating, alcohol, our body image, etc.?

The first step is to notice.

Staying with the process and finding a good supportive therapist or coach, if that feels right for you, to help ease your way through the challenges can help. It can help unravel the negative stories we hold about ourselves and the deep memories that limit us.

Identifying Your Triggers

When I work with people, I teach them to become conscious of their body: to notice any distress in it, how their body feels in certain situations and what triggers this reactivity. When we were children, we wanted to keep safe and if we sensed we were in danger in any way then the 'flight or fight' response kicked in. As adults, this same response will happen when a situation in the present reminds us of a past negative experience. Tuning into the body can alert us to when an old wound has been touched, thus showing us that we are not in the present.

Here is where some inner work is needed. Noticing and accessing the trigger points and coming to recognise the feelings constitutes the first step – to suspend the story that you are putting onto the situation and to go into the feeling in the body.

It helps to breathe deeply, to still the mind, to drop between the thoughts and to suspend time, allowing the feeling to leave the body. This practice, done regularly, can stop us projecting the past onto the current situation. The inner work can write over the old unhelpful memories and beliefs and we can operate in the here and now to create positive new stories that better support the preferred future and the life we want to lead.

Doing the work can create shifts which mean life is lighter, brighter and clearer - once the wounds have healed and the stuff from the past is released.

A Girlfriend for a Year Diaries: Part Five

Day 38: Tuesday 18th June. *If anyone can do it, we can*

My journey with Anadi was continuing. Today, we shared an email exchange that was open – and open-hearted. Anadi opened by responding to the comments I had made over the weekend, about seeing and sharing. (As before, I have left our exchange unedited, to allow the full exchange to be seen.)

Hello beautiful,

Thank you for your lovely text. I am so happy to be 'the one' that embraces your 'seeing' in relationship. I want to know ALL of you and I really do not want you to feel you have to shut down any part of YOU.

I really do understand it feeling stressful to say things that you see to me; I completely get that! I also understand more and more about breaking connection with you. That has NEVER been my intention, as we know, it is an adaptation that is out-dated and not needed any more. I am working hard to be free of this and I thank you for your help. You seeing is NOT too much for 'our' normal life and I really do not want you to feel like you are in prison because you can't say what you feel!!! That is NOT what my love is about. I want you to be all that you are, beautiful. I LOVE YOU!

I also understand that you have been 'waiting' for me to emotionally exit. That's what has happened in the past so why wouldn't it happen again? I'll tell you why, because I want this! I want to be with you and I want US to be all we can be, together! I will continue to open more and more. As I have already said, I have spent my life looking for you!!! Now I have found you I realise there is more work to do and that is fine. It is more than fine, I love our journey and I am excited to see how this flower blossoms over the years.

I am sorry you are exhausted, beautiful. We need to find a way of making our lives together more sustainable – if anyone can do it, we can.

I love you, I love you, I love you xxx

I responded almost immediately, feeling uplifted by his words.

Hello my darling Anadi,

I loved reading this email from you. It is exciting to think that you truly do want to deepen and open and grow together with me. I have woken up feeling rested and well! And I look very well too :) I have a Facebook message from a client: 'Inspired by your tantra video... the bluebell man re-emerged, a part of me that has been missing for a while. Bless you...' I am so glad that what we are offering is reaching people. I am really looking forward to making another one this coming weekend!

I love the unfolding, the being still and trusting that going within and doing the inner work is all that is required. I can feel everything emerging and I notice how the energy shifts around to create a lifestyle that helps support growth. I notice how it is through deeply listening and daring to express from that place that the growth and the truth really occurs.

I can see and I understand a lot at a deeper level, that being brought up within the kind of environment and social constraints that I have it has been an on-going journey to truly embrace my true nature, but with you I am being encouraged to do just that in a way that I never have before. Thank you, thank you, beautiful soul.

I know a few things and I am following those:

I know that I must make the space for us to spend time together, I know I must run, and from those two places everything is unfolding as it is meant to.

I am running with Matt in five minutes and then I am meeting my friend Sheila, for the first time since her husband died in March.

I love you darling beautiful Anadi.

With all my love, Julia Chi Xxxxxx

I loved running along the seafront with Matt – the sea was beautiful. An amazing pool of golden light was shining on it and it was magnificent. It came down from behind a cloud, translucent and bright, arcing out and creating a shimmering pool of beauty.

There was a message from Anadi waiting for me on my return.

Hello beautiful girlfriend,

I think our journey together is very exciting, I truly am excited to open up more and more and deepen and grow with you. I feel blessed to be on this path with you, I feel like I have waited my whole life for this.

I am so pleased you have woken up feeling rested and looking well – I was a bit worried! I knew you would be OK but I am aware that you have been pushing it a bit on the resting front.

I am also happy that our videos are touching people. I love that we are creating these together and that we are helping just by being us.

I think we are both encouraging each other to embrace our true natures, thank you beautiful Julia Chi. I would like to know more how I can encourage you in this.

I want to spend as much time with you as I can, I know we both have work, etc. but it is never long enough being with you, even Morocco flew by. I am so happy that you feel you must make space for us, I really do think it will all work out – I say that because we both want the same things and that energy has to manifest into something for us.

Enjoy your full-on day beautiful and I want you to know that you truly are the love of my life.

I LOVE YOU xxx

I felt optimistic and almost in a rush to get to the next stage in my life. While I realised that wasn't very Zen and in the moment, I was starting to really see the destinations ahead and the possibilities for growth and movement.

As always I was called to run.

As always I was called to go deeply into relationship.

96

Everything was emerging from this place, because it was the place where I was asked to be truly me and true to me – always.

I met my friend Sheila – my 'twin' – for supper. We first met her when I was 29, just about to turn 30 - she was 45 on the same day that I was 30. We drank Champagne in the Jacuzzi in the morning at Buxted Park and in the evening I had a party in the bar downstairs. I was dancing on the table when Sheila appeared, in a red dress. She had been dining upstairs and had come to see what I was up to. I beckoned to her to join me on the table, which she did. Her husband Terry, a president at American Express, had appeared in the doorway and given her what can only be described as 'the look'. Sheila had hesitated, but I said 'Stay, stay' – and she did!

She and Terry were happily married for 36 years, closer than ever in recent years as they had enjoyed Terry's retirement together.

'Wow' I said, 'It's amazing Sheila, 36 years. How did you do it?'

'I wasn't hurt like you have been.' she said.

It was interesting to me to see my pain reflected back: the pain that has made relationships with men a place of challenge and heartbreak, but of course growth too.

Terry died suddenly earlier this year, and it was the first time I had seen Sheila since.

Sheila is an amazing spirit and we had a wonderful evening together. She told me about how much she missed Terry, and of the gaps: in the morning from when she woke up at 6am until her aqua fit class at 9; and being alone in the evenings. She also spoke of the cruise she had booked, the elephant she would ride for seven hours – 'I've booked it!' she said. Within all of her plans, there was the endless missing, grief, and sadness showing through her laughter and her enthusiasm for life.

I walked home and Anadi texted me, thanking me for the card I had sent him. Then he said, 'I would call but I am cooking', and in that one sentence, that one little thing, I fell through into the hole where I feel unimportant.

I experienced the pain of my own losses and my own grief, mirrored in Sheila's, and triggered by Anadi's text.

Day 39: Wednesday 19th June. *If you can feel it you can heal it...*

The pain in my heart lasted through the night and most of today. Somehow my fears of loss and separation had been activated in the mirror of my friend's loss, and in her courage facing it. It was a real struggle. My heart was hurting and I felt too sensitive for this world. The poem *Invictus* by William Ernest Henley helps me a lot when I feel like this, and I found myself focussing on its last line: 'I am the master of my fate: I am the captain of my soul.'

Anadi and I spoke at lunchtime. He listened to me and he heard me. I assured him this was not to do with him - it was all about my own pain, and the way that I felt had to be a good thing, as it was an opportunity to release it.

Anadi sought to reassure me:

'I am not going to leave you and I am not going to hurt you. I love you with all my heart. I have never loved anyone the way I love you and there is no one on this planet I could ever love the way I love you because there is something very special and amazing about our connection. I value our love and connection and what we are doing beyond everything because what we have is like nothing I have ever experienced...'

If you can feel it you can heal it...

Day 40: Thursday 20th June. *Life becomes therapy*

Anadi and I spent another day texting each other, between everyday life. He was clearly remaining open to the process:

I feel like I have been processing all night, in an amazingly positive way. Looking at lots of areas where I have tensions and relaxing them. Really amazing I am doing this consciously while asleep. I feel very spaced out at the moment, like I have just had therapy :-) I miss waking up with you beautiful.

I felt drawn to acknowledge this:

I am so looking forward to being in your arms again – and in your bed kissing you and entwined with you! Overnight therapy is good! Choosing me for a girlfriend does actually mean that life becomes therapy! :) You may have realised this! You feel more relaxed on the phone, just this week. It feels it's been a big week for us again!

Anadi responded, validating my words.

I can't wait to be entwined with you again. I have realised that choosing you as my girlfriend means that life is one big therapy room. That is part of what I have been looking for, and to have our levels of intimacy, love and connection. I am more relaxed, thank you my love. I am becoming more and more aware of the areas I am not relaxed – they then relax. Oh – it has been a massive week for us – so much deepening. So much healing, so much love. I can't tell you how much I love you – totally and with all my heart.

It was safe to say my mood was shifting as we communicated, freely and with open hearts.

Hello my darling, I was just going to text you! I love all you have written in your texts. I love our journey and that I truly am living in relationship with you – what I dreamed was possible with a man – now I find it is! Amy reminded me yesterday that I said last year that I really would like a boyfriend that I could do things with like theatre and dinner out and holidays! I did say that!

It really felt as if Anadi and I were on the same page when I read his reply.

I love, love, love being in a relationship with you. I so dreamed of this and now you have arrived and we are here. So you said to Amy that you wanted a boyfriend – consciousness heard us – I said I wanted a girlfriend. I hope you are having a brilliant day beautiful.

I had to tell him the way that I felt.

Well, I didn't really believe the someone I was looking for was out there, but I did like the idea of having a best friend type person who was a boy. I didn't imagine I would want to give up the other men or that I would find what I have in you my beautiful amazing full-time full-on boyfriend! So this is more than I asked for! Better and brighter and bigger!

With every message he sent, I felt more loved.

Yay, I like better and brighter and bigger. And I love being your full-time full-on boyfriend. I love you beautiful.

By the end of the day, all trace of the previous day's mood had passed.

Day 44: Monday 24th June. *I was discovering that I was as willing to be seen as to see*

After a busy day with clients, I finally had time to write and reflect on a magical weekend with Anadi. On Day 41 of my year of being a girlfriend, I drove up to London after working with back-to-back clients. Unlike last Friday when the roads were chocka, this week it seemed there was a tail-wind. I packed too much because I couldn't think straight, and arrived after a smooth and swift journey with enough clothes for about five weeks.

I returned with many less, as I found myself putting some of the clothes in 'my drawers' in Anadi's bedroom and left my still-drying running kit for the next time I returned. I saw it as more than just a practical/sensible solution to avoid regular 'bag packing': a sign that my soul wants to be with him all the time.

In truth my heart and soul had become entwined with him and so being apart was becoming more and more of a wrench. But as we both explored over the weekend, we decided we still wanted to do this 'girlfriend for a year' – hopefully 'girlfriend forever' – in our own way. We intended to keep it fresh and alive, and the gaps apart certainly ensured this. They also meant that when I was working I was working and fully connected and concentrating, and when I saw Anadi, I was fully there, present and connected with no stress or pull. So, in truth, it felt good.

If it was possible, we fell even more in love over the weekend. The connection felt deeper and our lovemaking reflected this. Anadi commented on my eyes again, saying they were like beacons that saw through him. He imagined men might have run from them before, run from being so naked before me, so seen, so transparent. It made sense to me, as I had experienced men opening to me, then withdrawing and shutting down.

I had never been so keen to make love with a man, loved doing it so much, felt so totally present and connected, so 'turned on', or experienced my body being so responsive. Considering sex has been very high on my priority list of 'things to do' in life, this told me a lot about Anadi. The relaxation together seemed to increase and, with that, a space so vast between us that felt safe and open and had depths and heights that we had yet to explore.

We 'did' things together this weekend – aside from simply staying in bed! On Saturday, we met Andy in the park and ran intervals, fast and in step. Anadi had become so much fitter in the six months of unexpectedly being on a running journey with me, which seemed to have come as part of the deal of hooking up with me. Of course, he didn't have to run with me. But he'd become fitter than he'd been in eight years by default.

Returning home to a hot bath together before eating a delicious omelette Anadi prepared felt like an expansive and connected way to spend the mornings together. By now, we had managed to break the early habit in our relationship of staying in bed all day. Now we got up in time to run at 10am and return to bed for the afternoon!

On Saturday we got ourselves up to record some videos for Anadi's business. I made my instruction videos, then we recorded our Dialogue of Exploration video on the 'inner game' of sport, before shooting out to Islington for a delicious meal in a vegetarian restaurant.

I loved being with Anadi in the restaurant, the buzz of people all around us; tasty, beautifully presented food; a cocktail that went to my head in a delightful way. But the latter also accessed some insecurity, as often happens – though with it the positive side of feeling fearful, the awareness of this process opening me to greater wholeness, showing me that more and more I was trusting myself to be transparent and naked before Anadi.

I was discovering that I was as willing to be seen as to see. It felt good, Chi flowing freely between us and opening us to everything we could possibly be and experience; opening us to experience what it felt like to truly love another and to feel that love return.

Day 51: Monday 1st July. *They would feed me well and keep me safe in the bosom of the tribe*

Anadi and I spent the weekend meeting each other's family. First, we visited my sister Rosy, her husband Nick, and children, Jamie and Jess, who was performing in Bugsy Malone: the reason for our trip. On Saturday morning, we'd run along the seafront in beautiful sunshine, looking over a sparkling sea lapping at the edges of Weymouth bay, and bunting was everywhere. Were we missing a national event? Rosy reminded us later that the Olympic sailing had taken place there last year and so the bunting remained, reminding them of their weeks of fame, Olympic ideal and gold medals beckoning. As we ran, the colourful bunting represented limitless possibility waving and dancing in the morning breeze. We ran five half mile repeats and returned to our guest house feeling very sweaty and hungry.

Being with my sister was a happy time. Within an hour of arriving. a jamming session started and Jamie and Anadi were playing guitar together while Rosy and I sang and Jess found the lyrics and chords on her iPad and scrolled up the page for Anadi. I had a cocktail, which meant that as we walked up to the school for the performance I was, if the truth be told, a 'few sheets to the wind'. But watching the show was a delight. Jess embraced each part she played and was fully in character. Being on stage is her dream and I could see its unfolding in process. As we left Rosy told me that Jamie had said about Anadi: 'I strongly approve'. It felt as if Anadi was now part of my family.

On Sunday, after a run to the sea together and a detour to the 'garden of rest' where my Dad's ashes are buried – 'so I am meeting Larry Armstrong too', Anadi commented – followed by a long, lingering breakfast, we set off for home, via Anadi's 'family'.

In his case it wasn't his brothers and sisters or childhood family that I met, but his 'blood brother' Meru along with Meru's partner, Lucy. Anadi met Meru, who's a decade older than him, when he was 19. They spent time in recording studios together and are as close as anyone can be. There is nothing that Anadi would not share with Meru.

We sat in their garden, drank tea and ate strawberries and cream. I really loved both Meru and Lucy, and rapidly felt as if they were my family too. Meru has the same birthday as me, so we decided an event must happen to celebrate together. This plan in itself was the sign of the commitment to my inclusion and a recognition of the eternal nature of Anadi's and my relationship. I was a girlfriend for a year forever, the start of the year renewing moment by moment, it seemed.

Feeling so connected to 'my family' was strange, but I felt as if they remained with me after we parted: as if they really took me in as 'one of them', almost like they had been waiting for me and now that I had arrived they would feed me well and keep me safe in the bosom of the tribe. It felt good. I knew that we might not meet up again for many months, but it didn't matter, because I was one of them now.

Day 52: Tuesday 2nd July. *I felt tearful and afraid*

Anadi stayed with me after our weekend away meeting family and friends, until this morning. On Monday lunchtime he and I went for lunch. I felt that I didn't ever want to be parted from him, and yet I felt tearful and afraid about taking another step towards a commitment to our being together.

'What do you see for us?' I asked.

'I see that we are' he replied.

We had spoken about living together when we came back from Morocco, but after initial enthusiasm – as this felt where my heart called me – I had resisted, scared of the relating between us dying because of too much pressure within all that we are both committed to. Afraid of tiredness setting in and the spiral down towards disconnection and disappointment that I feared so much. So I had turned away from a mooted date in July when we planned that we would be moving in together. Now, my body asked that I take this step. It was July 1st and my unconscious remembered the commitment made in May. It seemed to me now that ignoring the pull towards moving in together would be going against where my soul and heart are guiding me, towards where my biggest learning and growth lay and the biggest reflection of love and consciousness.

Truth and love reflected in the face of another human being: love is all there is and if we refuse and turn away from an invitation to experience it more deeply, this is in truth a turning away from self and from consciousness – and therefore from love itself. And so I faced my fear.

On Tuesday morning, Anadi drove back to London, as he had meetings to attend to, but on Wednesday evening he came back. We made a new bedroom for ourselves in the roof, like a little tree-house, and the bedroom became Anadi's office and another living area.

We went out for a celebratory cocktail and came home to make love in our little haven, our cosy tree-house. Anadi and I felt that we'd discovered a true companion in one another and so, in the words of Marc Cohen: we went up to bed where 'with wild abandon we made love to our true companion'.

We got up on Thursday morning and ran for an hour around the Hollow and along the seafront. It felt like being on holiday. The next two days were the busiest days imaginable for us to start sharing our living space but it worked with ease. Neither of us could hear the other and we were able to fully engage in what we had to do. My clients and I could not hear him and he could not hear us.

Day 56: Saturday 6th July. *We laughed and gasped with the glorious contrast*

We woke up to a sunny day with clear blue skies and, after coffee and cuddling, ran eleven miles over the downs. The sun scorched down and Eastbourne had become a holiday town; everyone out in summer clothes, the ice cream kiosk doing a roaring trade, people out to feel the warmth on their faces and summer in their hearts.

We ran back along the seafront. Anadi said he felt like a dip in the ocean and so we did just that, icy cold and exhilarating. We laughed and gasped with the glorious contrast.

As we approached the bandstand, I heard music. I followed the sound and we became part of the crowd of uninvited guests gathered around the railings looking into the bowl of the bandstand at a wedding. We watched the lovers exchange their vows and their rings and listened to a poem about true love that encouraged the other to be all that they could be, in particular by being themselves.

Day 57: Sunday 7th July. *Limitless and boundless relating with consciousness at the very heart*

On Friday evening Anadi and I recorded another of our videos. This time we spoke about conscious relating.

To truly go deeper into consciousness, I believe that instead of leaving the body, it is about being consciously in the body and relating to others authentically and truthfully, honouring always the spaces between us where the relationships exist.

Anadi and I had committed to being in relationship in the most authentic and deeply real way – loving each other by being truthful to one another about who we were and daring to always share and be open about what was really occurring. This way we could both feel safe and go deeper and deeper into a limitless and boundless relating with consciousness at the very heart. We had been on a big journey over the past six months. And now, I was to go on another journey - without him.

As I flew away to the sun of Lanzarote with Pru, my friend Ange's daughter, for a week of 'boot camp' in Club La Santa, it felt like I had pressed pause and I had the space to reflect on an incredible journey to date. As the pilot announced we were flying over the Bay of Biscay, I opened a little notebook of mine filled with quotes and sayings that resonate with me. The last entry was written on January 12th, after Anadi and I found our hearts opening so completely to one another. Anadi had said, 'I will cherish you and look after you and treat you like a goddess'.

I found myself thinking that I had been on a journey that had seen me fall more and more deeply in love with Anadi, but had also tested us both to honour the commitment to authenticity and truth that we had promised, in ways neither of us had anticipated. The more I lived like this, within my being and within relationship with other people and the planet itself, the less I felt equipped for a 'normal' existence within society; and yet it seemed that I was also experiencing more, being invited to touch and taste this incredible human experience in new and exciting ways.

Day 58: Monday 8th July. *It felt like a physical wrench to be apart but my heart was singing*

Pru and I completed day one of the 'training camp' that is Club La Santa! We slept long and deeply and were rather blurry as we made our way to breakfast. By 9.30 we had collected the tokens we needed to take advantage of the facilities, and the 'system' was coming back to me from previous visits.

We made our way to the bike centre, hired a bike for Pru and headed out with me running and her cycling. The weather was still, quiet and cloudy, a pregnant atmosphere, calm in contrast to the rocky volcanic energy surrounding us.

As I ran I was aware of Anadi and of my heart connected to his, of the connection stretching into infinity, consciousness itself. Love, as I had long believed it was possible to express, receive and experience. Having spent ten days together, I felt a physical wrench at being apart but my heart was singing and I felt totally happy with our decision to live together. Distance and time apart to reflect would bring up questions and doubts if there were any, but all I felt was a commitment deepening with every minute that passed, and a feeling of moving towards him. It was no surprise that we had chosen to make our video on conscious relating last Friday, July 5th: six months and a day from when we first made love together.

The first day at Club la Santa was a great success; lots of exercise, sun, smoothies and salads and fun. The only thing that marginally marred it was that, as I went to clean my teeth, my right index finger knocked against the basin and it hurt. I had a small cut on it. I didn't think much of it, though I did notice that it went a bit red after it had been knocked.

Day 59: Tuesday 9th July. *I missed Anadi*

I woke early today to run in the half marathon. I had chosen to run it as a way of training, to do a long run. But even though I took it easy, it seemed much harder work than I would have anticipated. I also noticed that my finger was quite sore and red, and as the day progressed seemed to get worse.

I booked a sports massage for 5pm and, though the massage was wonderful, when I emerged my finger had worsened considerably. I suspected that the sports massage had sent an infection around my body, as I felt an escalated intensity of pain and swelling straight after. I showed Pru and the two of us went to 'sports booking' to ask for help. At first they thought I had gone because of my tiny cut!

'You're a delicate flower,' one of the Santa team laughed. 'We have people in here cut from head to toe having fallen off their bikes!' I explained it wasn't the cut I was worried about, but that something felt wrong. Was there a doctor who could help me?

I missed Anadi.

Day 60: Wednesday 10th July. *Anadi was helpful simply by 'being there', and loving me*

Sitting in the pool bar with Pru, I felt a bit weak. My finger injury had spiralled quickly into a painful infected experience. I knew it wasn't looking great – or feeling great – so Pru and I went to the doctor, who showed us how the infection had already travelled from my finger halfway up my forearm. He gave me some antibiotics.

It hurt a lot all night and so at 1.30am I got up. I was hot and sweaty and nearly fainted. I lay on the sofa and called Anadi who was love itself, 'there' and reassuring. Rather than talk mobile to mobile, I suggested I go to a wifi hotspot and we could talk on

Skype. I walked through a sleeping Club La Santa, resembling the Marie Celeste, without a soul about. It dawned on me there might be someone I could ask for help at reception. I was much relieved to find a night receptionist on duty. He gave me some painkillers and a bottle of water.

I called Anadi on Skype and I saw him naked and beautiful there, through the wonders of technology. My heart went out to lovers who have been parted with no way of communicating but through the soul connection, no way to see or hear the other, to be connected over long distances through the energy fields that we have learnt to tune into. We talked for half an hour in the silent empty reception area, usually so full of people.

The painkillers worked and I went back to bed and slept till 7am. More painkillers took me through the morning. It interested me to see how willing I was to use the wonders of modern medicine when I need to, and how vulnerable the body is.

Pru and I had a quiet day of rest. She chopped up my breakfast fruit and my lunchtime salad and accompanied me to the doctor, who took one look at my arm and said, 'Fuck'! The infection had spread further and I had a fever. He gave me more antibiotics and asked me to see him again at 8am the next day.

Anadi was wonderful, there at the end of the text as much as possible, even though he was in meetings all day long. He said he felt helpless. I understood that feeling, but Anadi was helpful simply by 'being there' and loving me.

Day 61: Thursday 11th July. *It was my turn to feel helpless*

It was my turn to feel helpless, after learning that Anadi's friend, Derek, was dying. The day before, Anadi had received a message to this effect and learned that had requested only his parents were with him at the end, but somehow this didn't resonate with Anadi. He was so sad, but I was 'here' and he was 'there'.

110

By now, my right hand was in a sling and I had to write my diary with one finger of my left hand. The weather was glorious and hot and though I had come here to train, I was doing less exercise than in a long time. But I felt relaxed and surrendered to accepting my infection, however long it might take to heal.

I visited the doctor this morning and then called Anadi. We were missing each other a lot and I truly felt as if we were twin flames.

Day 63: Saturday 13th July. *We could be together even when parted*

I was beginning to feel better. I felt as if I had turned the corner towards feeling well again, and my enthusiasm for life had returned. I even jogged a rather weak two miles with Pru in the morning and did some stretching in the gym in the afternoon. I looked longingly at the pool while she swam up and down, rather than feeling glad for a chance to sit quietly, as I had all week. Pru and I laughed a lot, about random things that girls together laugh about – with of course the hilarity of the moment completely lost in any re-telling to another person. Dr Antonio gave me hand exercises to start mobilising its use again.

We came back up to the apartment after breakfast and there was a text from Anadi saying that he had woken to the news that Derek was no longer with us. He was very upset and I called him straight away. I stood on the balcony with the sun high and blazing in a blue sky, sparkling on the sea below, and listened to him speak of his dear friend, of how much he would miss him and of his deep sorrow. My heart went out to him. I felt a long way away, miles across the ocean I was looking at.

After we spoke yesterday, Anadi had contacted Derek's nearest and dearest about his feeling that Derek would not have wanted him to stay away. They had told him that a short visit would be good, and so he had driven to Hungerford and spent precious time where the veil between death and life is thin, so thin as to not be seen at all. It is visible with clarity for whoever dares to truly look, and Anadi was that person.

He was able to suspend his own heavy heart and open his eternal soul to Derek, easing his passing by showing him that we are always connected through the eternal life of our consciousness; that if we dare, we can always see this in the eyes of a human being: there is love and truth and eternal life reflected. Anadi looked into Derek's eyes and they were able to communicate in love.

The biggest gift we can give another human being is to love them unconditionally: to connect with them fully, nothing held back, and give ourselves fully, but also let them go. To be capable of doing this when a person we love and we will never see again is dying is a rare ability, but it is also the biggest gift we can give. Anadi had driven to Hungerford and given this gift to Derek, his true friend who he had connected with over ten years and who he loved deeply. He showed him how loved and safe he was, that he saw him and his true being - and he let him go.

Anadi and I talked on the phone once he had returned home. Once again I said a silent prayer – no, make that a 'shout out' – for modern technology and how it connected us all so immediately. We could talk with the miles between us in an instant and experience the power of the human voice to connect our hearts and to share our love, our grief, our sadness, our happiness: we could be together even when parted. I felt like crying too, but in the same way Anadi knew not to cry yesterday when he was with Derek, I knew it wasn't for me to cry now.

Before I went to bed, I called Anadi from the balcony with the stars so bright in the sky, and we spoke about how far we had travelled in six short months.

Understanding the Process: Letting Go

To truly love anyone we must 'let them go' – to be themselves. Of course, we can make arrangements in business and in marriage, and in any coming-together of people. Groups of people need 'rules' and agreements to function well. But the higher the self-esteem and the clearer each person is, the easier it is to make up the rules and agree, and the easier it is to be truthful and engage fully with one another.

To truly hear the truth of another person, we must let them go, because at some point the relationship is going to end – even if through death. Letting go is about being fully with someone and not taking it personally if they decide to go, even if it is personal. So at the deepest level we must let go of our own life, truly recognise that we are dying and will die. This way it is easier to hold no one and have no expectations; so that if the rules have to be changed or the deal broken, then we have already let go.

Derek wanted Anadi at his death because Anadi could hold that space. Anadi could be totally emotionally connected to Derek, and also let him leave his body: help him let go of the physical connection and friendship and sharing we are all part of on this planet. Anadi told me that 'When Derek told me he was going to die I knew this was an opportunity for him to do so consciously; without fear or expectation. I was also aware that for Derek to have the space to do this, he would need someone who could let go of their own sadness and loss and be clear. When I went to see Derek I asked him, 'you do know this is your opportunity to become the Buddha?' This was a term we had previously used to mean die consciously. Derek nodded. I was with him twelve hours before he left his body and we sat in silence; the connection between us undisturbed. There were no emotions, feelings of 'not wanting this to happen' - we were both

113

clear, as a very wise Indian Guru once said to me: 'not a ripple on the lake'.

Anadi's Perspective

Having committed to being in a relationship with me, there were times when Julia felt that she couldn't 'do relationship'. Even though we had shared the deepest intimacies, cleared and healed so many of our childhood wounds and been completely open and vulnerable with each other, when Julia said she couldn't be in a relationship my only option was to let her go. As much as I loved being in it, I had no desire to 'hold on' to Julia or our relationship; even if I had it would have limited our intimacy and eroded our relationship. The times Julia felt she couldn't do this my response was always 'so what do we do now'.

I had felt very restricted growing up, and I was a very inquisitive and curious child. I would question why I was not allowed to do something and the usual response – 'because I said so' – was not enough. I would have to find out for myself, often leading me to getting into trouble. Later in life this led to me rebelling on a big scale. I could not be restricted or held and I had no desire to restrict or hold.

I wanted to be in this relationship with Julia and I wanted her to be in this relationship. The fact that she felt she 'couldn't do it' was hard. I had found in Julia the woman I had dreamed of and had come to the conclusion I would never find. So her wanting to pull away, once again, touched my 'someone I loved is being torn away' button. Of course, this time I was able to work through these feelings and this pattern by being open with Julia and talking it through. This was a new experience for me, I was very adept at working things out alone; yet here I was being fully open about what was going on for me.

Girlfriend for a Year Diaries: Part Six

Day 71: Sunday 21st July. *The time we shared was 'quality'*

For the first half of the previous week I was still ill from my infected finger, but as the week progressed, so did the length of my runs and my level of energy – my health was back to 98%, if not total 'wellness'.

Anadi and I were both working very hard and yet living together was making things better, not adding any stress, which had been my concern. I'd feared that living together, along with the amount of work I was doing and the desire to get up early in the morning and run, would squeeze out any quality time together. But the reverse was true. The time we shared *was* 'quality'. Even when we only had five minutes between clients, we still found time to connect and have a quick hug.

Anadi and I had discovered that being together was very nourishing, meaning that even though we were only sleeping for five or six hours at night, it seemed not to have an adverse effect on our well-being. I loved going to sleep in Anadi's arms. It felt like a place of total safety and nourishment and love. We made love a lot, even though the time for it seemed to have been reduced. The beauty of it outweighed any worry about the alarm going off sooner than we expected.

Today, Anadi and I went to his brother Stuart's home, for his daughter's 13th birthday BBQ with all the family. I met Anadi's Dad, Gran, brother Dave, sister-in-law Helen, and niece, Gaby. In the kitchen at one point, alone with Anadi, Stuart told him that he liked me, that I felt like one of the family and that Anadi had found a keeper.

The sun shone, and we sat on the grass, eating meat from the BBQ and delicious salads made by 'salad king', Stuart (recently trimmed down through going to the gym six times a week and eating salad every day). Seeing Anadi eating a sausage, burger and chicken after twelve years of being a vegetarian, his brother murmured to his Dad – 'it's the invasion of the body snatchers.'

I thought about how Anadi's attitude to food had changed over the course of our relationship. When we got lost in the mountains, it had taken so much out of us that Anadi didn't feel like he was recovering. He felt that the way to recover was to eat some chicken, and then a lamb tagine the next day. He said that he felt his body recover and thank him.

I told him that I had evolved a 'no rules' policy with food: part of the legacy of having had an eating disorder for many years in my younger days. I found that it helped me keep in touch with myself and my needs on a daily basis, and discovered that if I couldn't make choices about what I eat from a conscious place, it reflected in all other areas of my life.

Anadi liked my 'no rules policy': his new approach to food had emerged from getting lost and depleted in the mountains of Morocco. He continued to eat meat, chicken and fish if he wanted to; years and years of vegetarianism had disappeared.

Day 76: Fri 26th July. *I felt loved for all of me, with all my vibrant colours showing*

Living with Anadi has started to feel as if it was never any different; as if we have been this way for years and years.

On Wednesday we drove to Petersfield; I was having a session with Ros, my supervisor and therapist. I have been working with her since I was 32, often on the same issues, but clearing them at a deeper and deeper level.

In truth, we've always worked on the same issue: my healing from the self-hatred and the wound that meant I allowed myself to be abused in relationships. I believed deep down that I had to accept bad behaviour and be 'nice' at all times to maintain connection; that I had to 'shut up' to be able to have a deeply intimate relationship and get the love I longed for.

I had noticed this 'stuff' arising more frequently now that I was with Anadi. Although uncomfortable, it felt as if it was a good thing. If it was coming up then it was there anyway, even if hidden away, and I welcomed it. In coming up for healing, it could be let go of and I could be another step closer to clarity, more conscious and more free.

Last week, we went running one morning and I was particularly chatty and directive, I think. We were eating breakfast in the kitchen afterwards and Anadi said: 'I usually like being quiet when I run…'

Before he could finish his sentence, I reacted. I didn't let him finish. I had heard 'be quiet', and it hit a deep old childhood wound. By not allowing him to finish, I hit the same wound in him – being silenced and crushed. He managed to get through to me, by saying with energy, 'You didn't let me finish my sentence'. When he said it this way, with force, I stopped and I listened and I saw love in his eyes.

He was able to finish, and say that what I had been telling him on the run was of great value to him, and in truth he had used it to shift some of his own 'stuff'. It took me a while to shift the pain that had arisen by hearing 'be quiet' – even though this was not what he had been saying. My own projection still had the force of a real criticism. Once I had managed to shift this, I felt freer and lighter and clearer.

In my session with Ros we explored how, in this relationship, I had the chance to dissolve the wound that had led me to feel that I must earn love and connection by hiding part of myself.

With Anadi, I felt loved for all of me, with all my vibrant colours showing.

Day 81: Wednesday 31ˢᵗ July: *I was in a deep process of going into unreleased pain and hurt from the past*

I found myself using 'channelled writing' today, as I felt so ill and spaced out. For me, channelled writing entails 'getting out of the way' of any 'thinking' and allowing my right brain, intuition or higher self to answer questions. Put simply, I ask a question and write the answers down without any internal editing or 'thinking process'. The question might be as simple as 'Please give me insight and guidance into...' The practice has proved very accurate and if I listen to this wisdom, which can sometimes seem far away from 'conventional' thinking and ways of being, everything has always flowed. I asked:

Please give me insight into my body and why it is feeling ill.

My 'response' was: *'You are recovering from years of abuse; you are healing from the stress of trying to earn love; you are recovering from a big battle. Take it easy and allow the unfurling; allow the transformation. All is well'.*

This made me focus on the mind/body connection – something I have long been aware of, and have direct experience of. I met Tom on the May 4ᵗʰ 2006, and at the same time I developed a wart on my right index finger and on the middle finger. I treated them both with a freeze treatment from the pharmacy. The middle finger responded and healed, while the index finger reacted against the treatment and erupted. It scabbed over and then the scab came off to reveal an open crater of a wound. I tried many treatments, but each time the crater would reveal itself again.

Even at the time, I had a deep understanding that this was a process. Warts represent self-hatred and I was aware that my own self-hatred was revealing itself in the open wound, raw and painful. I had fallen in love with Tom and within a very short time, I knew that it was an abusive relationship at its deepest level; but it also filled me with joy and made me feel alive when I was in his company or even in email dialogue with him - he had amazing energy and talking with him stimulated me no end. He kept me on the back foot at all times while giving me just enough to keep me hanging on. I was addicted and could not break fully free – and all the time my finger kept on with its cycle.

Although there were breaks in our relating, I never truly moved on from Tom. In truth I kept hoping I could heal that deep wound *and* still be in relationship with him. And then I met Anadi. The love triangle existed until May 12th, when I fully committed to being a girlfriend for a year. I kind of expected my finger to totally heal, but it was still doing a mini cycle of its old pattern. The wound when it was open was very small, but it still opened.

After Anadi moved in with me, and Pru and I went to Club La Santa together, my wound was still a little bit open. I had been told that the different water infected it – but whatever the infection, it found its window in my open wound and I was very ill. However, when the infection left my body, the wound on my finger had healed – and has not opened since.

The immediate anger that felt directed towards Tom was now abating. I was glad of this, as anger feels horrible, eating up my body and my being: a curved sword that goes deeper within building hurt on hurt. While my nondescript illness was related to the antibiotics and the infection in physical terms, I felt that it was actually the release of the long held pain of abuse.

Day 82: Thursday 1st August. *Our connection grew deeper and the intimacy and relaxation expanded*

Today, I walked into the sunny street on my way to get a cake for my friend Ange. I felt happy and at ease, despite my 'not quite right' body. I still hadn't fully recovered from my injury at Club La Santa, but I was aware that I was in a deep process of going into unreleased pain and hurt from the past.

Anadi came home in the evening and I was so pleased to see him. We talked for hours and I found myself telling him about the bullying and torment at school when I was eight years old, then the daily misery of being bullied when I was twelve, all of which led swiftly and easily into my damaging relationship with my coach. Looking back, all the people who bullied or oppressed me, actually wanted me as their special friend. However, this is a strange way to be friends with someone – to try to trap them by crushing them. In doing so you lose what you were attracted to. By putting out their light, your own light dims too.

I could see the pain I had held on to over the years that was now holding me back. I was aware that I must release it so that I could be clear. The clearer I could become, the deeper Anadi and I could go, the more expansive my life could be, and the more capacity I could have to help others fly free too.

Anadi and I had chocolates, coffee, tea, banana and yoghurt for supper, then went to bed and made love. The art of sexual magic has always inspired and resonated with me. Sexual energy is the most powerful, creative and also healing energy: if harnessed and directed it can flow in all we do to positive ends. At orgasm we are totally connected to the energy of consciousness. The phrase, *petit mort* highlights the aspect of surrender, the connection to source and to one another. It isn't said lightly that one should 'be conscious of who you orgasm with'. It is a space of vulnerability and total openness.

121

To cast a sexual magic spell between a couple is a powerful creative exploration of all that you want to manifest. One aspect of 'sexual magic' entails creating a symbol which epitomises this and reflects all facets of this dream. At the point of orgasm, you both direct your sexual energy and imagine flooding the symbol with it, imbuing all you create with this sexual magic, so that your existence on the earth plane expands and deepens and reflects love and intimacy and magic at its most powerful and profound. As we made love, I said to Anadi, 'Think of our special symbol', and the energy of our lovemaking was powerful and deep. Our connection grew deeper and the intimacy and relaxation expanded.

Day 83: Friday 2nd August: *Run, Julia – run, run!*

This morning Anadi, Jim and I met for a 9 mile spin. Anadi and I ran to The Lamb for a 7.30am meet and the three of us ran up the hill, past the youth hostel, right to the top of the downs. It was a glorious summer morning and the runs in January and February, when we were so cold we could hardly think, were a distant memory and almost unimaginable. Now, with relaxed bronzed limbs, we were moving easily in the warmth of a new day being born.

It was the first time Jim and Anadi had met. They ran along chatting easily together and I heard Anadi saying that there was a time, not long ago, when he was going to bed at 6.30am, not getting up to run. We talked about how the choice of our friends influences our lifestyle. The relationship between Jim and I exists essentially on the run, and over the last eight months that Anadi and I had 'hung out together', Anadi had got fitter and fitter. At the same time, I had become accustomed to sometimes seeing the dawn before sleeping.

Anadi was strong enough to comfortably run along, sharing ideas with Jim and experiencing a meeting of minds with each running step. There was a moment when we were running along the peace path, high up over the sea. Anadi looked round to check where I was, and as he did so he missed his footing and his right foot went down off the path into nothing. He took what Jim described as a 'top tumble', rolled over a couple of times in the brambles and was back up on his feet in a trice - all of us laughing!

I found myself enjoying a space without a running goal as such. My intention was to keep working on balancing my body, 'going back to basics'. Without a race to prepare for, I found myself enjoying the space to keep working on the imbalance in my body, my weaker left side.

Jim described our Sunday runs as 'more than a run' because they offered a social time, a sharing time, a meeting of friends and a space for friendships to grow and deepen. I agreed, feeling keen to keep meeting them, and to keep being able to keep up, so that I could keep having the far-reaching conversations we all enjoyed.

I was conscious that all of my running friends were significantly younger than me and, other than Fi, my running friend of the past five years, all men. I felt mindful of looking after this body of mine, working on the imbalances, looking after it and celebrating its willingness to keep on running. Run, Julia – run, run!

After our run, Anadi and I had two days ahead of freedom and just us, no plans except to go to see The Tempest in the Italian Gardens on Saturday evening. Getting out of bed was a problem for us, even though it was sunny. We made it out running at 1.30pm on Saturday.

After running, Anadi had some work to do and I had some writing to do. He stayed at home and I went out for a coffee. I left him a note in the kitchen to suggest he joined me, if he could, when he was done. Just as I finished writing the last word of my blog he appeared behind me and hugged me.

Day 85: Sunday 4th August: *Within thirty minutes we had spiralled apart*

Our Sunday started late, so to 'get back on schedule', we decided to run for an hour only rather than two. As we reached the seafront I suggested we ran a mile fast, but relaxed. It was fun, it didn't feel hard at all, and we ran it in 6 minutes 45.

We decided to walk up the steps, and I heard music from the bandstand and wandered over, then stopped, sweat pouring off our bodies, to listen to a brass band playing Beatles songs. We moved back a bit so as not to be too sweaty a presence amongst the crowd and an elderly man suggested we stand by him. He then engaged us in conversation– me mainly, as I was beside him. We talked about sport and his four children, the eldest boy at 50 a marathon runner, the next down at 47, a tri-athlete and twin girls, one sporty, the other not interested all. He lived in Milton Keynes, as did his children. He had always loved sport himself and still enjoyed table tennis. His doctor was in full approval and encouraged him to keep playing.

I asked him if he had had a nice holiday.

'I'm going back tomorrow,' he said. 'It's not much fun on your own'.

I touched his hand and said 'I do understand'.

He wiped a tear away and was a little embarrassed. Anadi and I hesitated and he said, 'Thank you for talking to me'. I held his hand and said again 'I do understand'. He then went to hug me and after a quick warning from me – 'I'm very sweaty!' – he hugged me tight. I hugged him back and he said, 'You've made my day' and then made his way off into the crowd.

My heart hurt for a while. Anadi and I thought he was perhaps only recently bereaved. In that moment we were totally connected – I knew him. My hurting heart only accessed my own hurt and the interaction demonstrated to me keenly the need and the longing, the yearning for connection within us all.

Anadi and I finished the weekend feeling more connected and close and in love than we could imagine possible. We decided to go out for supper. I was sitting opposite him and I felt so relaxed and at ease.

I said, 'I have never felt so connected and in love and safe with anyone ever'.

Within thirty minutes we had spiralled apart.

In retrospect I can see that surrendering to that level, allowing myself that level of connection with a man, must have accessed fear within me. My body must have remembered so much disappointment in the past, men controlling me and never loving me as I needed to be loved, always wanting something from me. This is not to negate my previous relationships – we all did our best and could only understand and relate from the place we were in.

In Anadi, I had found my twin flame, but a chance comment – so insignificant that I cannot recall exactly what it was – spiralled us into a fight and it was the argument that hurt us, not the comment, both of us fighting from a position of feeling unheard, misunderstood and wrong.

We recovered the argument and by 2am were ostensibly 'fine'. We made love and woke up in the morning to a beautiful day and a beautiful nine mile run with Jim. But all week, something wasn't quite right. We fell straight into a busy week and were both aware that there was a disconnection.

Day 87: Tuesday 6th August. *Creating a life together with Anadi felt very natural*

Today, I found myself preparing a meal for Anadi to come home. I had previously said that I didn't want to engage in 'wife-like' behaviour or be thinking about things domestic, but it seemed so natural to finish work and walk up the road to get some food.

Maybe I was always in the wrong place before, in the illusion of marriage and playing a part, adhering to a script. I watched my mother and behaved accordingly with the men I married before, playing the part completely and losing myself in the process. Yet creating a life together with Anadi felt very natural.

Day 90: Friday 9th August: *We had both been protecting our hearts and if that happens then separation occurs.*

On the way to London, we talked and talked. We had plenty of time, as we were in the car for seven hours. A big queue to the Dartford tunnel meant that at 8.45pm we were still miles from Camden, where we were meant to be seeing a play at 8.30pm. We gave up and had a lovely meal and I drank a Margarita that knocked me out.

I truly saw that we had both been protecting our hearts and that if that happens then separation occurs. Something shifted within me. We worked through this together and both opened our hearts again, experiencing a deeper level of trust and intimacy than before. The shift felt physical in that it was a relaxation, and emotionally we shared a feeling of more joy and passion.

Day 91: Saturday 10th August: *'I'm spoken for now,' I said, taking hold of Anadi's hand*

As soon as we woke, we made love and both of us could feel that the pain had gone, that the process was done. We resolved to make sure that we trusted more deeply and remembered that keeping open isn't dangerous, that in fact not keeping open was what would hurt us. It would halt our spiritual growth making us disconnect from one another.

Rather than lose myself in the relationship, I was finding more of myself within the relating and the space between us.

We ran up to the Hollow, when suddenly I heard a shout: 'Julia! Julia!' I turned and there was my friend Colin, waving from the other side of the road. He came running over the road to me, followed more slowly by another friend, Tony. They were two of the founder members of 'Utopia Runners', a club which I set up in 1989.

Colin held me in a tight embrace and they regaled Anadi with stories of days gone by, a stream of men chasing me through Buxted Park.

'We hear you're available again,' Colin commented.

'No, I'm spoken for now,' I said, taking hold of Anadi's hand.

After one of Anadi's special omelettes, we made our way to his Dad's for a cup of tea. Anadi's Granny had put lovely bright clothes on for our visit. As we drove away, Anadi said 'I have never seen my Dad like that with anyone'. I could see how happy his dad was to connect with Anadi and I, and loved our time there.

In the evening we visited his old friends Hari and Yogi. Hari said she was so relieved when she found I was bubbly and not serious, and the evening flowed with ease over delicious amazing colourful food prepared by Yogi.

Day 92: Sunday 11th August: *It felt good and connected and special with Anadi there too*

Today, we called in on my Auntie Helen, en-route to Gatwick; I was so glad to introduce Anadi to her. I said he was my boyfriend and that I wanted her to meet him, before feeding her her meal. It felt good and connected and special with Anadi there too.

He and I had amazing sex in our airport hotel until about 2am, feeling more deeply connected than before. At 4am, our alarm went off. We were up and off, breakfasting early before making our way to the gate and boarding the plane for Santorini.

Day 93: Monday 12th August. *Now I felt that I was 'back' – another process*

Anadi and I switched between sleeping and talking on the plane: about marriage, about being a girlfriend for a year, and then another year, and another year, moving into marriage seamlessly.

On Friday morning I hadn't want to marry. All week I had been pulling away. Both of us had felt bereft but we stayed with the pain of separation. A small misunderstanding had tumbled us both into feeling 'wrong', as if we had 'ruined' something. So often when a couple are in conflict, it is hard to see the growth that is so wanting to blossom and it is also hard to see that both of you feel the same; are experiencing the same; are even saying the same thing. Now I felt that I was 'back' – another process.

When we arrived in Santorini, we walked straight to the beach and drank virgin cocktails in the bar, watching the sunshine fade. The woman who served us told us that she works there from 4pm till 1am, seven days a week from May through to October, when she returns to Athens. She used to work in Athens during the winter months, but since the crisis, it had become harder to find work. Her eyes filled with tears when she told us her story and we were struck by the power of group consciousness, and the attitude and pain within the feelings of dis-empowerment: the deep exhaustion of working hard to stand still.

We returned to our hotel to find that the island had been flung into disarray and darkness. There had been a fire at the power station and the main generator was destroyed. A new one was being fitted and men from Athens and Rhodes had been called in to help.

We went up the road to get something to eat. We found Dimitri's restaurant, ate Greek salad and chicken from the grill and drank beer in the darkness, lit only by candles.

Understanding the Process:
Conflict, Growth, Reacting and Withdrawing

My training as an Imago Theory Educator (a form of therapy devised by Harville Hendrix) taught me that conflict is growth waiting to happen. Whenever we experience conflict – whether that is within ourselves or within a relationship with another person – growth is wanting to happen. If we operate within this paradigm, transformation and magic can occur in all areas of our lives.

This means being aware of every reactivity within our body (which is always from the past; unless it is clean, clear pure emotion in the present, which feels different and uncomplicated). When we react to the words of another or a situation, we can identify that we are reacting to the past because the reactivity is often out of proportion to what has occurred. This can be seen in the car with 'road rage', or all manner of 'small things' that we react to with energy.

If we pay attention and listen to the tone in our voice, this too can alert us to 'stuff' from the past. And if we commit to conscious relating, and to becoming conscious ourselves of what we need to clear, then we will truly welcome 'conflict' as a way of growing and becoming whole.

When we react in the here and now, up to 90% of our reaction could be from back in the past – 'little' or 'childhood' us responding to the person in front of us as if they were our mother/father/sister/brother/teacher. We project onto that person because something has been said or done that has triggered a memory from the past and we have heard something different to what was actually said. We need to understand that here, some stuff from the past is coming up to be let go of and with the right mind-set we can heal our wounds.

Growth and 'Growing Up'

To be in conscious relationship we need to become aware of our childhood agenda and become curious as to where we have been wounded: where our needs were not met; what we most needed and did not get. This way, we can take responsibility for becoming whole and truly adult, rather than just, 'a grown-up', walking around with a wounded child within who can react at any moment to the present as if it were the past.

If we respond as a child rather than an adult, it maintains the cycles of pain and the limiting patterns, as well as often getting re-wounded and re-wounding others in the process.

Conflict is growth wanting to happen, so it is important to stay with it and commit to working through the pain and exploring it, rather than reacting to it or against it.

Reacting and Withdrawing

Whenever we react, we withdraw love, and shut down a little. This can happen when we feel our own hurt and sense of 'unloveability', lack of worth, or feelings of being unheard or misunderstood, if we don't work though them or explore them with the other, then as a way of (false) protection we shut down – and in so doing withdraw love from the other. They may then also react to our reaction.

What happened in my relationship with Anadi demonstrated this. The trigger was that Anadi felt disappointed that I was going to work over the weekend when I had said I would be free. We were in a restaurant, feeling very relaxed and close, and I reacted to his disappointment – or actually, I reacted to my own projection that he was saying I was wrong for doing what I said I wouldn't. My 'wrong' button got touched, and then Anadi's 'not being heard' button got touched because I reacted and didn't give him time to adjust. Once we were in the spiral, we both felt hurt.

These 'processes' tended to happen every time I was feeling most relaxed and connected. With them came such a hugely different energy to the one we had been experiencing and we couldn't seem to unravel the withdrawal that was occurring in front of us.

Anadi didn't 'react' to me working: he was just disappointed and I reacted before he had a chance to process. Once I had reacted, he didn't feel heard. In this instance, although we made up quite quickly, we retracted something and didn't open again; until we really truly explored it and saw our 'protection' mechanism had kicked in.

Recognise Your Projections

It is so vital when a couple are in a relationship to know that so much of our reactions are projections from the past. We may have heard something completely different to what our partner actually said – i.e. I 'heard' 'You bad girl, you are not honouring your word, you are wrong,' when what Anadi actually expressed was mild disappointment at my commitment to work over our own plans (He was probably in fact justified to more of a reaction than that!).

Once we have heard something from our past, we will often then go into our 'adaptation' – in my case, I generally feel very bad, apologetic, and withdraw – which is exactly what happened.

So often both people are experiencing the same thing, but then exist in separate spaces as they react to each other in the present through their own pasts, feeling that the space between them is no longer safe. This happened to Anadi and I, both of us withdrawing to the space we knew, our own spaces where we felt 'safe'.

Live and Learn

What we learned through this process was that this withdrawal diluted our relating and left us less happy and less connected. We discovered that the way to keep ourselves safe in relationship was to truthfully share everything that was going on for us, however hard that felt at times. We made a commitment to sharing absolutely everything, always, e.g. if we were out on social occasions and didn't enjoy it, if we felt attracted to someone, or felt sadness for the loss of a previous relationship. This way we could keep ourselves safe and also keep the space between us safe.

Anadi and I discovered the paradox: that by trying to protect our hearts we achieved the opposite in our relating: we were less connected. The solution to the problem then instead became the problem.

Many people try to protect themselves, especially their heart, to somehow stay 'in one piece' and to feel safe and to feel in charge. However, the more we close down to protect ourselves the more we cannot connect with others, let alone ourselves, and so we end up feeling more unsafe and more lonely.

Intentional Dialogue

A helpful tool to share with one another is the 'intentional dialogue' created by Harville Hendrix. It ensures that the person is heard and their position validated and empathised with and it also keeps the space safe by managing reactivity.

The technique of Intentional Dialogue was created to help couples stay present with one another and to prevent projection of the past onto the current situation. It creates a safe space for couples to explore sometimes difficult situations or emotions and allows for the reactivity, that comes from a wounded place, to be held.

The dialogue can be used with any relationship and in any situation. If a couple practice it with a non-emotive subject and with a coach or therapist holding the space at first, it can become a very powerful tool for them to really heal the wounds from the past and to create a safe space where they can re-connect and find the passion and trust they first knew.

Having a Dialogue

The format begins by agreeing to have a dialogue and deciding who will be the sender and who the receiver. The sender then speaks about whatever they wish to discuss and the receiver listens and mirrors back what is being said, repeating it as a, 'flat mirror,' so using the same words that their partner has, and checking if what they heard is accurate is important.

The receiver might say: 'What I heard you say was…', 'Did I get it…?' and 'Is there more…?'

When the sender has said all they want to say – and it is best to make it a dialogue, so avoid it being too long for the receiver to follow– then the receiver repeats a synopsis of what they have heard and checks it is accurate. This validates the sender.

The receiver then steps into their world and sees it how they see it, even if they find this a stretch. They might say, 'It makes sense you would feel this, given that…', 'I understand what you are saying…', or, 'I see that given your experiences you would feel…'

Then they empathise: 'I imagine you are feeling…?'

The sender then adds if they are feeling anything more, or perhaps something different.

Next, it is time to swap round and repeat the process with the receiver responding and the sender listening.

It is important that both people stay mindful to keep the space safe and allow for growth to emerge from any conflict that has occurred.

By recognising what we are hearing, and really listening to each other rather than our 'wounded child', we can move on from past pain and really relate with each other.

Anadi's Perspective:
Intimacy within Love. Love within Consciousness. Consciousness within Intimacy

Intimacy within love. To be truly intimate with another means having a trust that we are safe regardless of our vulnerabilities, insecurities and fears. True intimacy means diving into our vulnerabilities, insecurities and fears, and sharing these special spaces with another. This can take immense courage, depending on how wounded we are, and this courage is never stronger than when we love another, are in love or feel loved by another. Love really does conquer all!

When two people come together in love and consciously decide to be completely intimate with each other the most profound healing is possible. Creating a space of trust and acceptance allows for intimacy to grow deeper – allowing for more love, more trust and acceptance and therefore more intimacy, creating an ever-deepening, ever-expanding cycle. The more we can let go of outcome and agenda, the deeper we can go, the more healing is possible and the more conscious we can become.

Love within consciousness. It is very natural for us to fall in love. This, though, often means losing ourselves and not being conscious. Our lover has made us feel like we are the most important person in the world and we feel like we can fly. This love is usually based on a projection that the other is making everything alright and this projection therefore is unsustainable. These love affairs can end in very dramatic ways, leaving resentment and ill feeling.

If during the 'honeymoon' period we can maintain a sense of self – and by this I mean a sense of our conscious self – we open up to a richer, more real and sustainable love. Love flowing from consciousness has no agenda or expectation, it simply flows. Conscious love has no limits. It never ends and is not dependent on the other being a certain way. Love from consciousness is ever-flowing, spontaneous and always nourishing, not only for ourselves but for our partner and everyone around us. When we rest consciously in love we can't help but affect those around us, especially those we are in some sort of relationship with.

Consciousness within intimacy. The more conscious we are the more open we are to sharing and experiencing intimacy, and of course, the more intimate we are the more conscious we can become. Being conscious, or allowing who we are to be expressions of consciousness, means letting go of our sense of who we are. This means being absolutely clear. As Zen masters have been saying for hundreds of years: 'let no dust settle on your mirror until you realise there is no mirror'. This does of course beg the question: what does being clear really mean? Being clear means we have resolved all of our insecurities, fears and reactions until we are completely transparent and there is nothing within us for anything to touch. It means developing a very deep knowing that everything that happens outside us is a reflection of what is going on inside us. If an insult is thrown there is nowhere for it to go. We know fully it is an expression of the other and we have invited it in. When we are really clear there is no invite!

It means that we can 'see' the truth in any situation without judgment or it having any effect on our stillness. Being clear is a true expression of consciousness and the more conscious we are the more intimate we can be, and the more consciously we can experience intimacy.

137

This is the greatest gift of being: to consciously share consciousness with another doing the same.

A Girlfriend for a Year Diaries: Part Seven

Day 94: Tuesday 13th August: *We felt free, happy and alive in the bright sunshine*

We woke to blazing sun over the sparkling Mediterranean Sea and, after a late breakfast of orange juice, coffee, eggs, bread and honey, we set off up the road. We had no idea where we were heading but the road took us to signs saying 'Ancient Thira', so we followed.

'Oh my!' Anadi said. 'Look at that road.'

I looked up and saw it winding its way up, up, up the side of the mountain.

We settled into a rhythm and the hairpins wound us to the top with relative ease. We allowed the mountain to carry us rather than fight it or push up it and soon we were at the top, looking out over the town we had come from and the vividly blue sea.

After paying a small fee to see the 'museum' in the open air of Ancient Thira, we brought a can of Coke which we drank swiftly, then continued on our way up the mountain through the ruins. It was magical: ancient Greek history and mythology all woven together with a shrine to Aphrodite and the remains of statues of Zeus and Athena looking out over the land, among the remains of temples and houses where people had once lived. We felt free, happy and alive in the bright sunshine, with warmth on our bodies and a breeze taking away the intensity of the rays of light.

After absorbing the energy of Ancient Thira, we ran down the mountain again and straight to the beach, into the sea. Anadi dived down like a dolphin and I followed him. We swam and swam, and I remembered how to relax and swim in the sea. It was wonderful to find I could keep my eyes open in the salty water and swim free like a fish without goggles. By the time we had swum and found somewhere for a Greek salad and bread, then walked back along the beach barefoot it was 6pm.

Day 95: Wednesday 14th August: *We had opened to a deeper merging with the sun, the sea and one another*

Day two of our holiday saw us wake a little earlier to the certainty of sun and the freedom of a day to do as we wished. We had breakfast on the balcony, talking and re-filling our coffee cups: something that brings me total happiness.

Maria came over and showed us a route that would take us inland to a town called Vothona, with houses that were caves. We set off gently, having learnt to run in this heat by relaxing and allowing our bodies to open and go at their own pace.

The sweat was pouring off us as we arrived in the town centre, where we bought a drink and asked the lady who served us about the caves. She directed us straight through the town and, as we reached the top of a hill, Anadi asked a man sitting in a big coach where the cave houses were. He pointed us towards a wall, leaning over it we saw an amazing rabbit warren of houses built into the rocks. There was a temple in the middle and a stillness and peace in the air around us.

Anadi suggested we try and run a big loop around the edge, as he could see another temple across the landscape. I hesitated only slightly. The hill looked steep, the sun was hot, the loop looked big. But once we were running again and our bodies were in their rhythm, I was happy to be travelling further.

We were passing a house and a man called out to us. We clambered up the wall by the side of his house and jumped onto his balcony. He was trying to move a generator, but he hadn't the strength and his mother was too old and frail to help – she showed a mouthful of gold teeth when she smiled. Anadi helped him down with the generator and she appeared from inside the house with orange juice and two glasses. We drank gratefully, then on we ran.

The bends on the road made us blind to oncoming cars, and beside us was land full of grape-vines. It looked as if we could run across it and meet the road further on. The terrain was sandy and rocky and at times there were steep drops to our left, reminding me of my habitual holiday adventures, but we clambered over walls and jumped across rocks.

A wild dog appeared, barking with energy that was rather jagged, and so we decided to take another route.

'Are bulls friendly?' Anadi asked, having spotted one before me.

'I think healthy respect is best,' I replied and we took a wide berth.

Soon, we were near the temple Anadi had seen, and on the road which would take us down and back. We stopped briefly at the temple. A woman got out of her car asking us for a Euro to buy water with as her card could not get money out of the 'magic wall' due to the power cut. Then, we headed back to the sea, and straight in. It felt warmer and our swimming felt stronger. Walking barefoot on the stones by the sea to our lunch my feet felt tender, slightly bruised from the running yesterday, but stronger in the underfoot too.

Eating Greek salad swimming in oil and vinegar and mopping it up with bread is my idea of the best lunch ever. To top it off, we were brought complimentary Ouzo and the alcohol coursed through me, highlighting how much we had opened to a deeper merging with the sun, the sea and one another.

Day 99: Saturday 17th August. *Letting go of illusions and discovering self-acceptance at the deepest level*

Today entailed an 'intrepid voyage' to the end of the island and back. The breeze was strong, as we'd been warned by Dmitri, who owned the restaurant we'd eaten at the night before. We set off 'early' – a 10am departure instead of 12.30pm or 1pm – as Oia was at the northern tip of the island, 15 miles away. We thought we would run there and perhaps get a taxi home.

Knowing the road to Vothonas made the first part of the journey, for me, swift and easy: for Anadi it was a different matter. Nursing a blister on the ball of his foot and tight calves meant it took him until we had nearly reached Fira, the capital, to really settle into his rhythm.

Fira was alive with people and shops, with the energy of the night's 'party time' still lingering in the holiday air. We ran up a cobbled street and a man standing at his restaurant door stopped us and suggested we came and ate with him. We told him we were running to Oia, and he directed us the quieter route, inviting us to 'come and eat with me later'.

We ran on, and the road wound up and up. Already the journey from Kamira to Fira had been a subtle climb all the way, and now the hills became steep and winding, and the sun rose in the sky. We had planned to have breakfast in Fira, but the hustle and bustle kept us running, looking for an out of town taverna. Instead of a taverna, we found just the winding road, ever-higher, with stunning views of the island and the sea sparkling below us.

As we ran past a garage, I suggested we stop and buy a drink. We consumed two cans of Coke at the garage, bought some water for our run, and the man who took our money showed us where we were on the map. We had covered two thirds of the route already. We hopefully thought that the road looked like it was going to start going downhill towards Oia.

Stunning views called us to stop and take them in as we ran, while the road wound its way round the side of the mountain. The traffic increased as we came closer to our destination.

It was 12.30pm when we arrived in the town, with white streets and white houses high above a port, and boats bobbing many feet below us. We stopped for lunch (having missed breakfast) at the first restaurant we found, drank more water and iced coffee and ate our Greek salad and chicken kebab with enjoyment. A couple from Australia chatted with us. Anadi had gone to the loo, and the man turned to me.

'Don't tell me you have really run the length of the island?'

'We have.'

Soon, the couple were planning us a trip to Australia. They spoke of beaches stretching for 17 kilometres for us to run along.

We have virtually no photographic evidence of our holiday, just a few photos on the beach near our hotel, because we headed off each day travelling light. We took nothing but the clothes we ran in (with a bikini underneath in my case) and carried some money for lunch, drinks, and chocolate. The man from Australia had five cameras and one he could take in the water with him. We needed him to be following us! Instead, the couple told us how to get to the sea: through the busy streets and down a long flight of cobbled steps. Two donkeys passed us on our way down these steps, coming up with folk on their back - the easiest way to get back, the woman said. We walked through a restaurant to the sandy path that took us to the rocks.

My dad passed away nineteen years ago to this day. He loved to swim, proud of his Cambridge Blue for swimming, and was still swimming regularly right up to his passing. Anadi and I dived into the welcoming sea and decided to swim a lap of the little island just off the shore. I felt that I was honouring my father's life swimming as he had loved to do, and in the sea as well – his spirit needed to be by the sea. He grew up by the ocean in Egypt and learned Arabic sitting on the beaches, squatting with the locals. I was born in Africa where my father spent 25 years, loving having the sea to sail on and swim in.

There was a rock twenty feet up which beckoned Anadi to leap off. We clambered up and looked over the edge, Anadi leapt. I felt the fear - but didn't do it anyway! Leaping off high places is not really my strength. I have the confidence that if my life depended on it, or if, like in the mountains, there was no other option, I would do it. But there was another option, to climb back down again, and I did just that.

The sun was getting lower in the sky and so we decided to head for home on foot instead of in a taxi. It felt like a true adventure. Anadi had seen a pathway across the cliffs, and we climbed back up the steps, fuelled ourselves at the top with chocolate and more Coke (the diet of athletes?) and set off for home.

We found the cliff path which took us all the way back to Fira, ran the downhills and flat bits and walked the uphills. On reaching Fira, we again passed the man standing in the street outside his restaurant. He expressed amazement at our intrepid journey, and we went inside to enjoy more water and another very welcome iced coffee – heaven!

The last part of the journey was a bit of a blur. The roads were alive with cars, motorbikes and scooters making their way into Fira for a Saturday night out. The sun was setting over the beautiful island and running the road the other way was disorientating – at times I didn't recognise it at all.

We returned home to our hotel at 8pm, ten hours after we had left. We were dusty and tired, and drank a carton of milk from the fridge in reception straight off. The nice lady, who works with Maria, gave it to us when she learnt of our adventure.

Day 100: Sunday 18th August: *Even our swim was more of a play*

We rested the day after our run to Oia and back. The day passed in a bit of a blur of exhaustion in both body and mind. Recovery is easy in a place with sun and sea, amazing Greek salads and beer, cocktails and sweet thick coffee.

The sea was full of waves too, so even our swim was more of a play. Afterwards with the sun setting and no one nearby, I gave Anadi a 'blow job on the beach' (and couldn't help but think it rather resembled the name of a cocktail, or two rolled into one!)

Day 101: Tues 20th August: *Wherever love and consciousness desires – we would go*

We felt recovered after our day of rest, and set off in the noontime sun to Ancient Thira, intending to run over the top to Perissa. We had loved the swimming there a few days ago and so thought we would repeat the experience.

As we traversed the rocky road down the other side of ancient Thira, we realised I had taken us on another path which wound around the side of the mountain and took us to an old locked-up church, white and silent, with bells hanging in its window. There were stone benches outside and the views stretched to the end of the island.

'We could get married here,' I said.

We made our way back to the path that took us onto the road to Perissa, went straight to the edge of the water and were soon swimming out to the buoy, over to a white boat and then to the rocks. Clambering up the side, it was evident that my rock clambering skills of childhood had started to re-emerge. I climbed higher than last time and dived into the deep Mediterranean Sea; Anadi stripped off his swimming trunks and dived in naked to join me. I was only wearing my bikini bottoms and resolved to do the same, but a family of Americans had spotted our rocks and were swimming towards us.

We were hungry anyway so swam back to the boat, then buoy and back to shore to a very welcome omelette, Greek salad and water for me, beer for Anadi, and a sweet Greek coffee to totally restore me for the homeward journey. Greek coffee is pretty 'hardcore', but I was coming to love it.

We set off home, feeling quite spaced out from our exertion - Anadi said he felt like he had smoked a joint. We walked back up the mountain exploring how much the space together and the silence and freedom had deepened us in conscious living, and how experiencing it with another soul was taking us deeper into the experience of conscious love. I asked Anadi to explain his experience of Tantric sex within our relating, and loved his words:

'**As well as enjoying the physical act immensely, there are a lot of other levels that you and I freely explore. The fact that we are so open intimately means we can dive deeply into each other's expression of love. The gaps between thoughts can widen, allowing consciousness to shine. The more this consciousness shines, the more the gaps between the thoughts widen and so our lovemaking becomes the ultimate meditation: two lovers experiencing consciousness together.** Experiencing meditation in this way allows us to carry it into everyday life, especially as you and I are consciously doing this, which means that our daily lives become more and more of a meditation. We have to recognise, within this, that the mind and the ego are going to feel threatened and so will rise more vehemently to try to maintain their place in our lives. Of course, as conscious beings, we allow these just to pass through, without attachment or judgement, leaving us once again to be fully conscious.'

We reached the top of the mountain and were intending to run down the winding road to home when I was suddenly attracted to a rocky pathway I saw that linked one hairpin to the next. Anadi followed me down, and we saw that there was another pathway for the next hairpin, and another. After that, it became less obvious that a path linked the two bits of the road, but we went anyway and carved our own track. The tracks well and truly ran out after a while, but the adventurers within us were ignited. We could see that there was a way down, which had not been travelled, but beckoned us anyway. It was such fun, reminding us both of days gone by in childhood.

'There is no one else on the planet who would do this with me,' Anadi commented, as we slipped and clambered our way down.

We found a huge piece of lava rock and, with both of us holding it in our hands I felt the energy coursing deep into my very being. Near the bottom we came upon a beautiful tree, different to all the rest. Its bark was smooth and golden and its branches wound about in an unusual way, with big frond-like leaves. It was different, magical, and I put my arms around it and hugged it to me tightly. Anadi came and hugged me and we were like wild free children, dusty and alone on the side of a mountain.

We reached the road and bought lemonade and chocolate with whole almonds in, which we ate on the beach, then walked home along the seafront, past the restaurants luring folk in to dine. Not one person asked us into their restaurant, looking like castaways as we did. But they did engage and one man put his fingers up in the peace sign as we passed. 'Peace and love!' he called after us.

Anadi suggested that we do a ritual to honour our commitment to a life of love and consciousness, and we came to the decision to draw our special symbol on a rock facing the moon; the symbol represents the creativity within us, our true path of conscious living – our life unfolding before us.

'A life of love and consciousness and we are totally supported in this.'

We bought water in the supermarket and bluey-purple nail varnish to use to draw our symbol on a rock. On the way home we practised with a tiny one on the wall and a bigger one on a flat broken tile in a pile of rubble.

We returned home to our hotel, showered, and were about to get dressed to go down to the rocks for our ritual and then dinner when we started to make love on the bed.

'Let's go onto the balcony and make love under the moonlight,' I said.

Anadi put a few towels down on the stone floor of the balcony and we went outside.

'You're beautiful,' Anadi whispered to me, looking deep into my eyes as we made love under the special light of this special moon. 'My intention,' he continued 'is to be with you forever.'

We were slightly disturbed by our neighbour coming out onto his balcony! Anadi said that he caught sight of us, saw that we were naked and did what he had come outside to do before discreetly returning indoors. We dressed and made our way down to the beach.

Finding the rocks we had marked as the ones to paint our symbol on, we saw there was one that was bigger than all the rest, pointing upwards towards the sky, the front of it flat and catching the full rays of the sun by day and the moon by night. We clambered across the rocks and perched in front of the big one. The waves were splashing against the rocks below.

'I'm going to take my clothes off,' I said. I was naked in two minutes, crouched below our special rock; the spray from the waves landing on my bare skin. Anadi took his clothes off and joined me. I drew the symbol as best I could in the darkness lit by the full moon. Together we recited the words:

148

'We have created a life of love and consciousness, and we are totally supported in this.'

We put our clothes back on and walked to a restaurant with a table on the beach, positioned exactly with the moon shining down on it. We ordered Greek salad, beer, and Mexican chicken, and enjoyed the perfect meal. We were brought shimmering pink complimentary Ouzo which sent us deeper into an altered state. The magical energy felt limitless all around us, engulfing us and taking us. We understood now, that wherever love and consciousness desires – we would go.

Day 102: Wednesday 21st August. *The power of the full moon was working her magic already*

We both felt much shifted and the space has expanded within us. I felt so different within my being and Anadi said he felt the same. We woke quite early, just after eight, which meant that even with a leisurely breakfast, catching up with emails and writing, and enjoying glasses of orange juice and cups of coffee, we still headed out of Kamari before ten.

By now, we were very familiar with the hill to Ancient Thira, though this did not make it any easier. Up and up we climbed, until we were sitting on the wall at the top, gulping down a bottle of water and relishing a large juicy nectarine each. As we sat on the wall, I turned to Anadi and said: 'I love being a couple.'

'Well, you fought bloomin' hard enough not to be one!' he laughed.

It seemed a distant memory, that time back in March and April, when I fought so hard to be 'free', until our time away in Morocco in May when I committed to being his 'girlfriend for a year'.

We had passed a woman on the road, walking up as we ran. She had engaged with us when she arrived, and now she passed

149

us to make her way down the hill again. We chatted a bit, then she told us how much she liked being alone. She said this a few times, reiterating that she could do what she wanted when she wanted, with no one else to consider. I would have said the same thing not so long ago, and if we are alone, then it is best to love it, to accept and embrace it. Within her words though was the longing and yearning for connection, to be together and not alone, and so she had connected with us: a couple so very much representing togetherness and love and ease of doing whatever we wanted, when we wanted, with another.

We set off again, clambering down the rocky path and made our way to the church we had found the other day. After resting there a while we climbed up to the cave which Anadi had looked into when we were here before.

The nice lady who works with Maria had given us her torch and so we were able to walk right into the cave's mouth and under the smooth brown ceiling made of rocks; silent and cool and full of the energy of the volcano that had made it. Mission accomplished, we journeyed on to Perissa, where we planned to eat breakfast. The ocean beckoned us first and we swam to the buoy and then the boat and then back to the shore. After drying in the sun, we put on our clothes and went to our cafe for a Greek breakfast of omelette, toast, orange juice, coffee and yoghurt with honey.

Setting off again for Red Beach, our planned destination, was a bit of an effort. The sun had risen high in the sky and our stomachs were quite full. We walked up the road to the signpost to Fira as this was the road we knew we must take. My knee was quite sore, having challenged it hard with our descent down the mountain two days before; but it eased in and we ran up a steady incline until the road turned sharp left and the signposts led us to Red Beach.

The road to reach our destination had been sparse and evidence of tourists was not to be seen. But here was a different matter, we arrived to a busy energy. The crowds had gathered and as we walked over the cliffs to see Red Beach there below us. We decided to return to the rocks where there were no people and we could swim alone and be alone together.

As we walked away from the incredible dark red rocks that surrounded the bay, we passed a young woman selling jewellery, authentic stones and silver from mainland Greece. I saw a band of silver I liked, and Anadi energised it with his energy: 'without end or beginning'. We chatted to the young woman and bought the ring. As we left he slipped it on to my finger.

We swam again and noticed that we were quite weary. After drying again in the sun, we set off for home, walking two or three miles on the road to Perissa. Stopping for lunch, we were totally amazed to discover from the restaurateur that it was 5.15 pm – we had no idea it had got so late! The restaurant looked over the bay, with spectacular views of the island that we had come to know so well by travelling around on foot. We commented that photos are a funny thing – with all the airbrushing and such like that goes on with making models even more beautiful, so it is with the photos of Santorini. They had cleverly marketed the island this way, but it had a beauty and magic all of its own which seemed to us more real, more true and simple than the photos portrayed.

Getting home wasn't as hard as it had felt it might be, after arriving tired and hungry at a restaurant a long way from home. We were back and showering by 8.30pm. We planned to go to Dimitri's for our last supper. This is where our whole life took a totally new direction. The power of the full moon was working her magic already.

As a result of on-going intentional dialogue and conscious relating, we had come a long way. Back and forth we had travelled. I had not initially wanted to commit to exclusive relationship; it was what Anadi wanted with me. Anadi was expressing desires to buy a house; I didn't want to own anything. I had always seen marriage as the ultimate in a union of souls, Anadi had never believed in marriage and didn't see the need for it. Anadi wanted to spend more time travelling; I was worried about my work and resisted more time away…

Gradually the process of being entirely truthful through one-on-one authentic dialogue brought us to a place, over dinner in Dimitri's restaurant. A decision had been reached that the best path for both us would be to travel more, to experiment with going away for longer periods of time. There we were, sitting under the moonlight, drinking our beer, and it was me who said: 'If we are going to be away more, why do we need to have anywhere as a base? Why do we need a 'home' – when home can be wherever we are?'

And so a random comment from me about not really needing to have a fixed abode, and Anadi's reply – 'I'm up for that!' – led us to 'let go' of everything. When we returned, we intended to give away and sell everything we owned and start to live a free, nomadic lifestyle of love and consciousness.

Day 103: Thursday 22nd August. *What a lot had happened in 100 days!*

Back on May 14th we returned from Morocco – it was Day 3 for me of being a girlfriend for a year. Today we returned from Santorini on Day 103 of me a being girlfriend for a year. What a lot had happened in 100 days!

Day 109: Wednesday 28th August. *I would be there for my friends and my family, always there even if I was away*

I came back from Santorini to mega-work. It all felt a bit overwhelming: full-on work and letting go of everything, all at once. We'd been home for six days and our new lifestyle was unfolding. I'd cleared out a lot of 'stuff' from the flat. Family and friends had been told and no-one was very surprised.

Amy thought we were 'off' backpacking as nomads, abandoning everything; she felt sad that I might be going. It took me a while to realise that this is what she thought, but then I reassured her; that I was far from going, just freeing up a bit.

I told Jane of our plans in the kitchen while making a cup of coffee. I sensed something was wrong. She wept a bit and said, 'I don't want to lose you – but I don't want to hold you.' I reassured her that we would be back a lot, that she could fly out to wherever we were, and that I didn't want to lose her either. Rosy was very excited; Ange said it sounded like I felt free. I told Rob's mother, who said she didn't want to lose me. I said I would always be there for her. I couldn't be lost, I would be there for my friends and my family, always there even if I was away.

All these conversations made me really see that I needed some kind of base: even if just a room to work from, a place for people to find me, a place to come home to; a safe space. I wanted a space with ambience and colour to represent me, that people would recognise as mine – my sofas, some pictures, my bright throws and my blue pot with flowers in.

On Tuesday morning I ran 13 miles with Fi. It was brilliant to chat and catch up, not having seen one another for a whole month. She also said she didn't want to lose me and couldn't I have a base here? I told her I needed to have somewhere to work from. We talked about me renting her studio – perfect! We shook on the deal, and I told her about the moonlight ritual which began this whole life change.

The room happened within days and, equally quickly, I sold my car to Amy's mother, Leia. I became a regular with the folk in the charity shop a few doors up, appearing daily with black bags full of books and all sorts of things!

Anadi told many of his family and friends, who were unanimously supportive. 'I've always seen you doing this,' his sister said. A few commented that it was good he had someone else to do it with – 'Someone on the same track.'

And so we were to be nomads.

Day 111: Friday 30th August. *Anadi had swept away all the orbiting men*

On Friday morning, the alarm went off at 6.30am, heralding a run across the downs with Jim. I was feeling rather stripped bare and vulnerable, as the last 36 hours had seen me tumble through an unexpected process. Letting go of everything felt exciting and I had a desire to do it, but my body had shown that there was more going on within me than was showing on the outside. On Monday morning my tummy had awoken me at 4am, very upset, and I had 'trotted' back and forth to the loo and felt quite 'thin' all day.

I worked hard all day, back to back, and finished rather spaced out – but I was used to this. Anadi was away in London and so I worked on my emails until midnight. He returned at 12.30am and then we chatted and caught up for a couple of hours. It was lovely to hear about his conversations: one with his business partner, who was supportive and affirming about our plans; and a chat with his friend Kamran over a curry, who made a comment about the fact that Anadi had swept away all the orbiting men.

Day 118: Fri 6th September. *I felt clearer and happier than I could remember*

What a week! I felt clearer and happier than I could remember. Every day, I emptied the flat of more possessions. Initially, it seemed however much I cleared out it still felt messy and full of junk, cupboards over-spilling with useless stuff. But every day I took bags of rubbish and possessions to the dustbin or to the charity shop and it was really and truly happening. I was becoming a nomad with very few possessions. The flat was starting to feel light and clear, at last.

I ran with Rob today, and he liked our plan. He commented that he liked to have a base, but that he would envy me the holidays and the sun.

I later met Amy for a 'business meeting'. I like our meetings. They are creative and I get a clearer picture of my business. I had got to the stage where I did not want to sit in my room with people hour after hour, day after day. I wanted to live my life: being with Anadi, running, writing and having fun as well as working with people.

Anadi came and joined us at 2pm. He looked over my website, with my web-guy Dave, as we were completing finishing touches so that it could be a site that Amy could manage and be creative with. Dave and Anadi worked together on one sofa (the 'geek sofa') while Amy and I sat on the 'girl sofa' and planned flights to Costa Rica. Amy found an inexpensive flight that had a stopover in Miami, and Anadi alerted her to the fact that, due to his drug convictions, he was not welcome in America! 'Bad ass...' Dave piped up. The evening was full of laughter, friendship and creativity. All felt good.

Yesterday Fi and I formalised me renting her room for a year, to use to see clients when I am back. I viewed it on Monday. It was perfect, with its own entrance, parking, a space for my healing mat and Fi was getting a loo put in. It was, according to a client of mine, a good address too – the Harley Street of Eastbourne!

This week was a happy one for Anadi and I, flowing and full of ease. On Wednesday night I finished early and, after some supper, we wandered over to Hudson's for a cocktail, which was wonderful and zonked us both out. We sat chatting together and Anadi told me his story of an Ayahuasca ceremony where he took so much of the drug that he really did think he had, 'overdone it this time' and would have to let go of his own body alongside everything else he experienced letting go of during the experience: his friends, his brothers and sisters, his nieces, all his possessions. In that space he was aware of his consciousness, the eternal self that never dies, and was never born; the part that is, and is part of the whole of consciousness.

Later as we lay in bed, Anadi was stroking my body and I was in a half-sleep state. Suddenly, I said, 'I had to let go of you and I have'. I don't know where these words came from. They came unbidden from within me. Later, I woke in the night and asked Anadi if he was awake. 'I'm half asleep and awake,' he said, so I told him my waking thoughts. 'All the reactivity, all the pulling away, all the insecurity; it was all because I hadn't let you go...' We felt closer and more in love than ever. Deeper and deeper we went.

Day 120: Sunday 8th September. *The winds of change were whistling around us*

This morning, we met Rob, Jim, Flo, Rupert and Miriam at The Lamb to run, at 7.15am after last night going to bed at 10 something - a miracle! It was a glorious September morning and we covered 17 miles.

Anadi would not have imagined a year ago that he would be fit enough to run 17 miles and be living out of London, by the sea. I would not have imagined that I would be fully committed to a beautiful boyfriend who I would be taking off on a lifetime adventure with.

Anadi and I went for coffee and cake.

'I wonder where we are going?' Anadi said.

'Where are we going?' I responded.

We chatted about this for a while and decided that we would find out. All that was required of us was that we kept clearing and doing our inner work and the way would emerge.

Later, as Anadi played his guitar – a possession he thought he might keep – and I wrote, we had a text from Amy about our Costa Rica flights, which were almost booked. Fi had already sent me an email saying the room conversion process was all in motion. The winds of change were whistling around us.

I had been experiencing an anxiety about my clients leaving me, working with a feeling that I had to be 100% at their beck and call. I didn't know I had this within me, so it was an interesting process, but not a very hard one and I now felt clearer. Amy and I were fine-tuning and restructuring the business, to be more streamlined and easier to manage. I worked though vague money worries, vague anxieties, subtle trickles of fear flickering through my being about my business just vanishing away, no one coming to see me. These feeling took me more deeply into trusting the process and going where my inner being, my deepest self, was taking me.

Anadi was working with a few anxieties too, but essentially neither of us allowed them to take hold. The power of two felt a very strong force. I realise I had never properly experienced it with a man before.

We went for an Indian meal in the evening. I sat across from Anadi, who looked so clear and bright. We talked some more about our journey. We had felt close all day, and before coming out we had been making love on the sofa. As it wasn't the most comfortable place, so we'd decided to move up to the 'tree-house'. The energy was building and building, our bodies were hot and sweaty and deeper and deeper we went into one another's eyes, Anadi's were like big lagoons of consciousness and love: such depth. Suddenly I thought of our magic symbol – sexual energy coursing through it would give it the magic and power to keep taking us further into our journey of love and consciousness. 'Think of our symbol,' I said. As our orgasms built and the energy opened more and more I thought of the symbol, the symbol we had painted in blue nail varnish on the rock in Santorini. As we lay together in the peaceful aftermath of passionate sex, we said out loud together: 'We have created a life of love and consciousness and we are fully supported in this'.

We ate our meal and talked about our magical lovemaking experience. The trust was deeper, and the flutterings of fear and anxiety had left. All that was required was that we did our inner work, and kept clearing anything that blocked us from total self-love and connection.

We then went out for a cocktail. We were the only ones in the bar, and we sat on the sofa and drank our colourful drinks: my beautiful lime-coloured Margarita with the salt all around the edge of the glass and Anadi's pink Long Beach. We left the bar intending to lie in bed talking some more, instead we fell asleep with the light on and woke at 1am to turn it off and spend another night wrapped in one another's arms.

Day 122: Tuesday 10th September. *'We have created a life of love and consciousness and we are fully supported in this'*

I was nearly a third of the way through my first year of being a girlfriend for a year, and I liked it a lot. Today our flights came down in price by £400 and Amy booked them. Within an hour, Anadi's new passport had arrived by recorded delivery. The universe was supporting every shift we made. It reminded me of our mantra: 'We have created a life of love and consciousness and we are fully supported in this'.

Day 124: Thursday 12th September: *My curiosity often took me out of bounds...*

I travelled to Petersfield to meet Ros for a session. Our connection spans 22 years and she has had a huge influence on my development, both personal and professional. We worked with the on-going pervading sense of 'wrongness' within me which feels so out-dated: my own sense of my needs not being valid and even the way I choose to live my life not being honoured.

I had reached an 'enough' point with this and Ros sent me a piece of writing that touched me, using the metaphor of a trapeze artist drawing awe by skilfully 'using the gap'; she said that she thought of me as having grace and confidence.

She also suggested that when doing something off the radar of others, it sometimes helped to introduce the change by saying, 'Once again I am embarking on something that might not make sense to you...' It felt good to have that as a sentence stem: reassuring to me and a space that allowed me to introduce to others that they might not understand, rather than a space for me to project that I was wrong for taking the actions I was.

We explored that, as a little girl, instead of being 'naughty', I was simply exuberant and curious; and my curiosity often took me out of bounds. I like that too: exuberant, curious, passionate, full of grace and confidence. These qualities felt they would help me navigate the uncharted waters of my life and leap across the gap from one bar to the next.

Day 125: Friday 13th September. *This was as much a spiritual journey as a human one*

Last week Anadi and I made love twice in very intense fashion. It was a very magical space. Anadi's face changed before me into an 'other-worldly' being and he said that my eyes burned through him. Both times we remembered to hold the symbol we have created, that distilled our life journey in our minds.

'We have created a life of love and consciousness and we are fully supported in this'.

These words were comforting. As we leapt into the unknown, fears were still arising.

There is a gap between certainty and bewilderment, and Anadi and I were both in it. This space, this transition, this gap, did not exactly feel like bewilderment but it did feel like we were on the edge of a strange new world, where we didn't fully yet know its ways or its language. So Anadi and I were travelling out of bounds into new lands and uncharted territory with passionate, exuberant curiosity. I liked this new approach to the world. Every week it seemed that I was clearing some old pain: a process occurred, an episode that asked that I address the unresolved pain from my past. It sometimes felt tiring, but the more I was present to my feelings, and the more I cleared this pain from my being, the more my life opened and my relationship with Anadi deepened and the intimacy grew.

Today, Amy, Anadi and I went to see Fi's room and measure up. It was a lovely space and much bigger than it first seemed. Amy and I then had a meeting and we could see that the business was evolving and expanding from the inside out.

I then ran to Gildredge Park to train with Matt. We were working with elastic ropes and I loved the feeling of running against the resistance. I could feel that I was developing and improving and that the handstands I wanted to do, as I had as a child, would not be far off.

Anadi arrived to run with us, as we had planned. With him watching I wanted to impress a bit - old stuff from the days of Daddy and Tim (my coach). I was doing high knee lift work and my calf pulled suddenly, acutely! I knew it was hurt, but I still did two more runs with Matt. This was a mistake.

When it was time to go running with Anadi, I started off across the park.

'I can't run on this,' I said. I felt dizzy and out of it and then suddenly tearful.

'I'll go home with you,' Anadi said.

'No, you go.' I directed him on his run and I was emphatic; and yet I wanted him to mind-read, to stay with me and to look after me. But he honoured what I asked and ran away across the field.

'Do you want a lift Julia?' Matt called.

'No, thank you.'

I waved him off too, and then stood in the middle of the field watching Anadi's back going off into the distance and Matt's car driving away. I cried a bit and then limped home: I did it to myself!

In that vulnerable moment it felt safer to send them away myself rather than to risk them going. In truth it took all day to process the pain that had arisen, old pain, deep inside, old pain that had not arisen for a while – but now it did. It came up for healing and once again I was asked to stay with a process. I had been feeling so safe, so confident and at ease, totally relaxed and trusting of Anadi and I, and in a few moments I had dashed it to the ground. I realised I was not yet quite recovered. It went deep in to a place of wounding, a place so unsafe and vulnerable that I was left raw and exposed.

Ros had told me that what Anadi and I were doing asked that we became more dependent on one another. I wanted this. I wanted to learn how to surrender. This was as much a spiritual journey as a human one.

Even though I had a full day of work planned for the next day, Anadi and I went out to have cocktails and get some supper at The Loft, one of the livelier places in town. How I was enjoying discovering the joys of drinking! We had two cocktails each, which was plenty to make me feel delightfully drunk. We wandered next door to a restaurant in hope of a meal, but had been chatting for so long that we arrived way after the kitchens had closed.

At home, a miracle occurred: I whistled us up a meal, chopping and dicing and mixing and tasting. In no time we were sitting, eating my first re-emergence into the world of creative cooking. For ten years in my first marriage, I had sat up in bed on Sunday nights planning the meals for the week. I tried to be a good wife! I abandoned this role 20 years ago and although I had stuck with being an ace salad-maker, I had not wanted to venture back into the world of cooking – until now.

We went up to bed. If I have had a drink, it seems that words come unbidden from my lips. I was lying in a relaxed, tipsy state and suddenly said 'I am so looking forward to you meeting my brother'. The words came out of my mouth, but I didn't think them first. Anadi was massaging my legs and body and I said to him: 'I have always wanted to be with a man who did this to me…' I have no memory of saying those words but I trusted him when he told me I had.

Day 126: Saturday 14th September. *So far, none of my fears in relationship had been realised*

This afternoon, Anadi and I spent two hours formally working on his process, in my room, as a 'client'. Working formally in this way allowed us the time and energy to unravel aspects and delve into his patterns and processes; to see where his wounds were holding him back, where healing was needed. He said that it churned him up, and me expressing my fears meant that his arose too. But we were united in welcoming any ripple to the surface of the lake. To be clear and present, we must see where the fear takes us away from living in the moment and demonstrates where we are not conscious.

Anadi and I have been reminded again and again to trust the process, to leap anyway, and to find that we are supported and safe and loved. As John Burroughs said, 'Leap and the net will appear':

Taking off together with Anadi was taking a great leap of faith. My history had not given me the message that leaping with a man was a good plan. But leaping I was, and trusting that the net would appear. So far, none of my fears in relationship had been realised.

There was a timelessness to our energies when they were together. I still had a slight feeling when I am with Anadi of time never being enough, or at the end of the day the conversation broken rather than ended; the pause button being pressed before we continued again in the morning, waking in one another's arms for another day of being together, loving together.

On Saturday night we went for the supper we hadn't had on Friday. Over dinner, I asked him whether he had a 'plan' about marrying me.

'What's the plan?' I whispered again and again! And so he told me:

'Once the flat is sold, I am going to buy you the moonstone ring with the stars that you love and then take you to dinner at

163

the Mirabelle (lovely French restaurant in the Grand Hotel here in Eastbourne) and propose to you there.'

'No no, you're not supposed to tell me the whole plan!' I laughed. 'Now you'll have to make another!'

Day 127: Sunday 15th September: *It did take an effort when fear was present*

This morning, we woke up and I was aware that I was 'worrying' about money; about my clients not coming back if I had big gaps; about not being able to live our dream. I saw once again how 'easy' it was to be present and in the moment when everything was flowing with ease, but that it did take an effort when fear was present. I felt glad to challenge myself, to discover where there was fear. Anadi said the same.

Day 128: Monday 16th September. *We resolved to create more 'playtime' together*

Today, I had a wonderful 'play day', going to Lewes to meet Anna in the hydro pool for 'aqua rehabilitation'. I loved the timelessness and weightlessness of being moved through the pool in a watery meditation; surrendering to Anna. Being held by her and feeling my body opening and healing was a very transformational experience.

Anna had asked me what my 'goal' was when I first went to her. I had said to be able to do handstands again. I didn't really have a goal in mind, but in February this year, I had already said to Anadi that I had a mission to be able to do handstands and cartwheels again. Last session, in truth, my attempts to stand on my hands, even in water, were pretty poor. Anna had held me in the handstand stance so my body could start to relearn how to do them.

This time, I did two awesome handstands in the pool! The twelve year old within me came alive and my body remembered. I spent all of my time on my hands when I was that age. Afterwards, my body ached, and my ribs and shoulders hurt. I could feel the effects of the new movement, even though in the water it felt effortless.

I spent the rest of the afternoon with Jane, celebrating her birthday with beetroot and goat cheese salad, breads and oils, delicious banana chocolate cake and present-opening. We resolved to create more 'playtime' together.

I told my landlord of our plans. He was happy for me, wished me well, and said if I ever want to come back I was welcome.

Day 135: Monday 23rd September. *'You have worked so hard and now the light is here'*

So much happened in the last week: a big week with big shifts and a big process. As I finished typing my last entry, my left shoulder started to stiffen up in a very painful fashion. By the time Anadi arrived home I could hardly move it and it hurt a lot. Thank goodness for Kinesio tape: Anadi strapped me up, the pain subsided and I had a little bit of movement. The next day, though, it was impossible to move it. Amy arrived with her dad Michael to take the mattress and sofa away, and I wasn't much help.

My shoulder was sore all day and seemed to get worse, until the evening when suddenly it loosened and the pain lessened. I was sure it was a process because by Thursday I had full range of motion, by Saturday I could only feel it a little bit and on Sunday it was gone!

Even though I knew it was not the same, the fact that I had been paying out for flights, deposits on flats, and for most of the extra treats reminded of an old pattern of mine: draining myself of money and throwing my all in with a man, just to watch him leap to better things professionally and the relationship ending in tears and heartbreak, leaving me tired and with less money – alone but wiser! I had had enough of that pattern, it was long out of date. Noticing this did access fear within me, but once it came up and was released with some tears I could see it as the 'stuff' that it was – like being sick. Anadi said he sort of 'got off' on the stuff coming up within him; we both knew that more clarity and consciousness was always on the other side of process. Bring it on!

On Wednesday Anadi met with a client of mine, Steve. I saw possibilities between them that led to them agreeing that Steve would work with one of Anadi's software projects, setting up a team of people to help him.

On Thursday, Anadi heard that his business had won a major award, with investment to integrate its software with other management and monitoring systems. He and his partner were to be part of a team of ten developing software that would be used to build 'smart cities' – cities that used software to become more efficient, more economic and more environmentally friendly. Personal shifts and processes and 'I knew this was going to happen' are all interesting positions after the event.

Anadi and I drove to London on Friday night, tumbled into bed and made love then slept deeply before waking for a run in Trent Park with Andy. We told him we had booked Costa Rica, his suggestion; that Anadi had a 'plan'; and about the award. He was very happy for us.

On Saturday afternoon we went for birthday tea with Anadi's granny, who was 94 years old.

'There was always the light at the end of the tunnel, but it never got brighter' she said of Anadi and his dreams. 'You have worked so hard and now the light is here'. She was totally delighted.

Anadi called all his family in the evening, every one of them. His father cried, he was so delighted. There was so much healing for Anadi in his affirmation: and so much healing for Clive in his affirmation of his beautiful brilliant son.

Early on Sunday morning I woke up to go to the loo and, back in bed, lay pressed against Anadi's back, unable to sleep. I kissed his neck and he turned over and we made passionate gentle beautiful love as the sun glimmered through a grey September morning. We slept for another three hours and got up to run around the park again. The day turned glorious and sunny and we ran ten miles before coming home to an Anadi omelette special. I worked and he cleared some stuff out of his flat. Both our flats were getting emptier...

Day 146: Friday 4th October. *It felt like exciting times*

Only six weeks ago in Santorini, we made the decision to become nomadic and free of owning very much. Since then, we had let go of most of what we owned and Anadi had put his flat on the market. Last weekend we'd cleaned it from top to toe. I scrubbed the kitchen and bathroom in my pants and a vest top, as it was too hot to be fully dressed.

By the time we left on Sunday afternoon, the flat was transformed: empty, clear and gleaming and ready to go to its next 'owner'. My flat was also emptying of everything but the sofas, chairs and colourful throws and cushions I needed for my therapy room.

When we arrived in Mallorca we went in search of the centre for some lunch. Not atypically, we missed a turning, and in the heat of the afternoon sun – still dressed in our jeans from journeying from an October England – we walked and walked, until we eventually came upon a very quiet street with one tapas bar that was open and willing to give us lunch.

We ordered tapas and cold beer, and sat and talked, watching the locals come in to drink at the end of their day's work. No English was spoken to us, the food was exquisite and the beer delicious and refreshing, lending a magical spaced-out air to the afternoon, particularly after travelling on three hours sleep. We talked some more about our future and a decision that I had come to on the plane.

There was unrest in Anadi's company, between his business partner, and a third party who they had sold ten percent of their shares to and tasked with selling the company's software. As yet, there had been no sales which was leading to trouble in the camp. Anadi and I talked a lot about the relationships involved and Anadi did a formal development session about it with me. My suggestion resonated for him. He opened and allowed his spirit to grow more and more into all it could be, and to expand in the form of his creativity, manifested through his business.

I suggested I buy the shares from the third party. Once I had suggested it, it became the thing I wanted to do, to be part of Anadi's business, and engage my energy fully in the company. It felt exciting. To buy the shares felt right – 'if it is to be, it will be'. Anadi spoke to his partner, who was open to the idea, and there was a tone of relief and gratitude in his voice.

Day 147: Saturday 5th October. *Listening to our inner voice is all that is required*

Anadi and I spoke over a long, leisurely breakfast. We only just made it there, waking at 10am after a wonderful sleep. We talked about how things always 'let us go' in the end. Do the inner work; this is all that is required.

I would not have thought I would be committing so deeply to a man, risking the curtailing of my independent spirit, my feminine sexual expression, my creativity and my power. This had been the experience in other relationships with men, so it felt a risk for me. Instead, I was finding that I was opening to deeper and deeper expression and that all my fears were unfounded. When I explored my fears with Anadi, of feeling trapped, and of the pressure of relating, the exploring only served to free me, taking me deeper into myself and helping me see the vast vistas of possibility stretching ahead.

We spoke about how Anadi's music had fallen away and given him up, rather than him stopping it; and I said that I felt the same way about competing in running. When I was interviewed by Anadi back in December last year, I had spoken about how my journey towards running becoming a total meditation on the move entailed letting go of any attachment to an outcome or pressure from the stopwatch.

Since my knee injury in June 2011, when there had been a crack like a gunshot as I was running a half mile interval, I had been in a bigger process of letting go, or rather my competing days letting go of me. Immediately after it happened I had sat on the bench on the rain and accepted, 'this might be it'. That summer I spent every day in the sea, and one day as I walked up the beach, I had an epiphany: 'it's about letting go'. I knew that then, walked on, ran again within weeks and started to compete. Something big had shifted with every race I had run since. I had not felt nervous, I had just run and let out what was within.

In my interview with Anadi, I'd said that my next journey was to train for the Brighton Marathon, and to have no attachment to an outcome: to stay in the step and to accept whatever emerged. Little did I know then, that on January 4th we would together set off on our own journey as a couple, and that would mean my training for a marathon was not as it used to be! At 22 miles in the Brighton Marathon I had said to my body. 'That's it, you don't have to do this ever again.' Six months later, sitting in the Spanish sun with Anadi, I fully recognised that my running in competitions was done. The need had left me and I felt free to set off in other directions: to run in the sun free of pain and restriction, free as a bird, doing what I was born to do: to become running and let the running take me where it would rather than try to direct its course: to stay in each step and to let the pain and stress within my left side finally leave me, as I found out what I knew right at the start – that I didn't want to compete, that I hated competing, that I wanted to run free on the common.

I realised that I had said these words to my mother and father years ago, when I was fifteen years old. I read my mother's diary after she had died. This is what she had written on that day:

'We had a tear and a swear from J last night, poor little thing, she says she doesn't want to compete, hates competing, that she wants to run free on the common, but as Larry says, you can't have a concert pianist that doesn't perform and temperament is a bore; J will come through I am sure.'

And so I did come through, and forty years later I was allowing myself to run free, without competing, to run free on the downs. Or maybe competition itself was allowing me to go free.

Day 148: Sunday 6th October. Mallorca. *With space came big decisions and the opportunity for shifts and deepening*

Anadi and I were sitting under the trees outside our farmhouse hotel in the mountains of Mallorca. It was totally idyllic (thank you Amy). Last night, I dreamed that I had lost a small cat; a bit older than a kitten. I was searching for the cat and a man joined me to help me in my search. He led me to a building and down some steps and there, lying sleeping, was the cat. It had grown and was bigger than when I last saw it. It leapt up as I came into the room, came running to me at great speed and jumped into my arms.

I told Anadi about my dream and he looked up the significance of dreaming about cats. He told me, 'the cat represents an independent spirit, feminine sexuality, creativity and power'. This resonated with me. Since we arrived on Friday I had once more been working with my fears of being 'trapped and tied down' – none of which were actually happening in my relationship with Anadi.

In some ways I didn't see a way out. Maybe this was all part of being human? When we are in a relationship we want our 'freedom', to be footloose and fancy-free; and when we are 'single' and truly are footloose and fancy-free, then we are looking for a connection with depth and intimacy. Or maybe it was just me?

As we were flying in to land, I had a sense that I could make this weekend difficult because of what was rising up in me. My left hip had been troubled for two weeks now, extending within the buttock, which made running very hard and uncomfortable – so much so that I had done little running in the past two weeks.

Instead of making the weekend 'difficult', it gave us a space for exploration and truthful dialogue. Anadi continued to be open to us creating the space to explore and we talked deeply and openly about what was going on for us, within us; and what we both wanted to create in each moment for our future together as a couple, and also within our work and professional lives. With space came big decisions and the opportunity for shifts and deepening.

Day 149: Monday 7th October: *Freedom and love, different sides of the same coin...*

Today was Anadi's 47th birthday. We sat all day by the pool, moving easily from a long breakfast to the pool terrace a few metres away. We stayed there until about 4pm, when we decided it was time to walk to Port Soller for birthday cake and coffee.

We walked to a hotel with amazing cakes and cappuccinos, to sit and talk and watch the world go by. On the way into town we spoke about our missions here on earth: about how the levels of consciousness we experienced had led us to one another and ultimately to support one another in a bigger expansiveness of consciousness on the planet: through our work and being, through my activity and through Anadi's stillness; and through the stillness within my activity and the activity within Anadi's stillness.

Later, we walked to another restaurant to eat dinner, then returned to drink a cocktail and dance on the pavement to live music outside the hotel. I danced a lot and felt free. Anadi joined me at the end, then we walked home through the night. The stars were so bright in the sky and we made deep connected passionate love together. Freedom and love, different sides of the same coin...

Day 150: Tuesday 8th October. *Freedom within love, love within freedom*

We were at the airport again, about to board the plane for home. Our time here had once again been transformational. Being with Anadi *is* transformational. Unbeknownst to me, the new moon in Libra was 'offering' all sorts of challenge in relationship. Of course, this can always lead to growth, but the experience of travelling through the current changes in my life, however transformational, were also hard and upsetting.

Now, at the airport and feeling clear and shifted, as always I felt grateful to the space that allowed me to process and heal. I was also full of gratitude for Anadi for staying still within the 'drama' of the very real – for me feelings of despair and self-hatred, within having 'got into something' that then felt wrong for me, and then despising myself for expressing what I felt and by doing so hurting another. I had nearly done five months now, of being a 'girlfriend for a year', and processes like the ones I'd been undergoing really made me glad that we are doing a year at a time. It would be really interesting to review and truthfully explore where we wanted to go next, on May 12th 2014.

Most of the weekend though, we'd had a happy time, relaxing and talking, making love, eating and drinking. My hip was sore, still playing up, and so running was no fun.

Once back home in Eastbourne, over a delicious Indian meal, we talked a lot about the weekend; about love and being conscious in relationship. We explored, again, how it was the first time that Anadi has not pulled for freedom in relationship, and how it seemed that we were acting out opposite sides of the same dynamic: fear of loss. I had been acting out the fear of loss of self, and Anadi had been acting out the fear of loss of the other. Different sides of the same coin. We committed again to learn how to live fully in love and consciousness, without fear of loss of ourselves or of the other. Freedom within love, love within freedom.

Understanding the Process: Keep on Working

I love experiencing the strength and vulnerability of the body at the same time. The tiredness and disorientation that comes with a long journey, coupled with continuing forward movement, is for me a powerful metaphor for the journey of life. The world keeps turning and we keep journeying, with our destinations ever-changing and moving as we strive towards different challenges and experiences. Yet all there really is in front of us is the next step, and then the next. All we can do is take that next step, keep getting up one more time than we fall, keep doing this even though nothing is really certain except the trust we have in ourselves and our deepest eternal self.

There are different doors along the corridor of life: shall I go through this one or that one? There are always choices and decisions to be made – or travelled through at any rate – in every moment, until we reach our final resting place where there are no more options and we surrender to letting go. The challenge seems, for me, to be about learning to let go in this lifetime, to truly surrender to the step we are in, to truly surrender to each moment.

In running, I have found a space where this surrender happens within the spaces of challenging journeys travelled. Whether adventuring with Anadi for the sake of the journey we have embarked on, or more formal challenges such as running a race and striving for an outcome, the challenge is still to stay in the step. It is all part of the same space that reveals more in every step. Letting go becomes about letting go of illusions and discovering self-acceptance at the deepest level.

Fear of the Future and Clinging to the Past

It is not always easy to let go, but the biggest causes of anxiety are fear about the future, and regret and sadness about past events and memories that have caused anguish. As humans we swiftly go to these places of anxiety. However, any new adventure, or any adventure that throws us off centre and creates a wobble, is to be welcomed: the wobble was already there, it has simply been revealed.

Every time our wounds are pricked and we do not process the pain out of the body, we cannot help but withdraw love a little. Together we can heal, interaction by interaction, noticing always our reactivity and endeavouring always to let go: of fear, of tension, of pain and anger, and clear the way for total love to flow in and out.

More and more, I see that time is irrelevant: it is human and part of the human journey, but 'things happen' almost on their own. It is simply our job to work with the stuff that blocks us from realising our potential, and to allow in what there is for us to experience. We must get out of the way of ourselves and trust at the deepest level.

Let It Go

Being brought up a Christian I have always been attracted to this quote from the Bible:

'Look at the birds of the air: they neither sow nor reap nor gather into barns, and yet your heavenly Father feeds them. Are you not of more value than they?'

My belief is that all that is required is to do the work of focusing on our own lessons and not those of others, and be responsible for how we see the world. All unfolds from this place, because everything is in relationship. By this I mean noticing 24/7 any reactivity within the body, which will point to some unresolved stress or tension from the past.

If we commit fully to clearing this, then what emerges is our own inner truth and wisdom, and if we follow this then nothing can 'go wrong' because we are on the path of becoming conscious and so in that place there are no energy blocks, only flow.

If we do hit a block in our life, then it is worth investigating where we are blocked or where the wound is still unhealed. The clearer, we are the more the flow. If we follow our intuition life will always work out – but we need to do 'the work' to be able to feel what is intuition, what is fear and what is 'stuff'. This, like everything, takes practice!

Core Work

Core work is work that goes into our very deep 'core beliefs'. In discovering what we are holding about ourselves and about life at the deepest level, we can then work to shift these deeply held orientations and beliefs if they do not support us.

Often people live their lives without examining them as they do not know they are operating from this place. It is only in working to explore and peel back the layers of beliefs and lived experience that we can discover what is holding us, what is supporting us, and what is limiting us.

My core fear has historically been that the man would exit from truly engaging in relating, and be unwilling to make the relationship sacred, the main priority. These fears were proving unfounded fears this time round. Everything that Anadi had done, said and been had deepened the relating; and everything he put into the space between us contributed to the safety and love in our relationship. I endeavoured to always do the same. My deepest knowing was that not leaping would cause confusion and was riot in the 'grand scheme', as it would be against the natural flow that was occurring.

Through doing the 'work' – working deeply on anything that blocks and holds us back, working to heal the wounds – through committing to consciousness in this way, life unfolds and there is no need to push, to force things to manifest.

The manifestation comes of itself, from within, from the deepest part of us, the part that is connected to consciousness and knows what we truly need and want for our life to unfold as it is meant to. Listening to our inner voice is all that is required, but this can be more of a challenge than we think, especially when the voice asks that we do the opposite to what we 'think' we want.

Working on Myself

As mentioned, I had looked out of the window as we came into land at Mallorca airport and had a flash of insight that our time there might be challenging. My flash of insight had proved to be accurate and, even with forewarning, I was unable to prevent the rising fear of being 'trapped' in relationship, a feeling of misery and abject unhappiness. It felt so real.

It continued in occasional waves over the weekend, so the time was not spoilt, although expressing my feelings of loss of self, dis-empowerment, and exhaustion 'due to' being in a relationship did feel incongruous with the abject beauty all about us: the sun, the tranquil farmhouse, the mountains rising around us as a backdrop, the delicious food - and me crying and miserable and feeling lost, alone and confused.

Anadi listened each time these feelings arose. Each time, they were released with the 'speaking out', the 'being heard', as well as his own non-reactivity and ability to understand me. He said it was the first time he had not himself had feelings of pulling away, of pulling for freedom in relationship. He told me about his time in India, when his meditation had reached such depths and such expansion that he felt then he had taken himself beyond relationship, beyond the possibility of meeting someone who would be willing to meet him.

I had felt the same before I met Anadi. I felt I understood my stuff that still needed clearing, but that I had taken myself beyond traditional relationship. Yet in being with Anadi, apart from being met in every way, which I never expected, I still experienced my own confusion, my difficulty being in a relationship because of my unhealed wounds, and the pain that frequently arose to be cleared could feel overwhelming for me. That weekend, that pain rose up in surges – to be released and cleared of course – but almost overwhelming surges all the same, seeming to me to cast a shadow over what could have been an idyllic weekend in every way.

Sometimes I didn't feel like it was 'stuff', so to speak, but that it was the dichotomy of my own being, just one of the contradictions I had to accept and live with.

On the eve of his birthday, my 'speech' about how wrong being in relationship felt for me did touch Anadi and his wound of loss and separation. My outpourings felt real to him, and he felt I saw no way out. This meant his heart became heavy, full of the unhealed grief of losses past.

I committed to riding through the processes in the future with more care of Anadi's sensitivity and of his heart. Maybe it was simply me; maybe I would always work with the discomfort of 'wanting to be single' within being in a committed relationship. Maybe there would always be times when the form felt as if it was a constraint and I would want to pull free. My wish was that I could feel free and that love could deepen within this, in all my relating. My work had much to offer humanity; Anadi's work had much to offer humanity. We had much to offer one another in our growth and our opening to greater levels of love and consciousness.

Love and Freedom

Osho says that love and freedom are different sides of the same coin. Try as I might, being in a committed relationship brought up feelings of restriction and slight anger within me. I felt I must restrain myself to be with the other, and often I saw no way for true freedom within this form. And yet, all relationship asks is that we consider the other, that we be kind, that we do not do or say anything that wounds.

Before I was a girlfriend, the feeling of freedom within myself was deep and real, but I had not found a person to connect with on this level, who could open deeply – or at least not without the commitment of being 'together'.

Ironically, the idea of 'being together' brought up for me more insecurity and expectation and reflection of myself within the experience of the other, than when I was not formally a girlfriend. The longer I was a girlfriend, and as the novelty of newness faded and Anadi and I became an item, the more I felt that my edge had gone and that a part of me was lost: a familiar pattern of feeling for me.

This, I could see, was my challenge: to be free and to be myself whilst being a girlfriend. Keep doing the work.

A Girlfriend for a Year Diaries: Part Eight

Day 156: Monday 14th October. *Everything was shifting and changing, opening and expanding*

The days since we'd returned from Mallorca had been good. They passed in a blur of working with people. I finished late on Wednesday and Thursday and Anadi and I sat and chatted over supper before falling into bed. The space in Mallorca allowed us to work more deeply with the fears both of us had over loss, and this week had seen us feeling different: more relaxed than before, closer than ever, more in love. It felt incredible that it could be this way, but that was the way it was.

We felt even more connected than before when we made love: deeper, more open, more expansive. I looked into Anadi's eyes when he was coming and he into mine and there lay a vastness that is beyond anything I had ever imagined. Deep down, I had always hoped something like this might be out there, in the energy field of another that was prepared to open to mine. Anadi again commented that my eyes are intense, they burn with it, he said. He also got an 'other-worldly' look to him when we made love; he looked different, but more himself than at any other time.

My running seemed to have let me go. I chose not to run all week. My body had hurt, particularly my hip and inner thigh. The pain had moved about and the idea of running had not appealed - so no running had happened. I did meet Jim for a coffee, for an hour. though I was glad to meet him and we resolved to keep meeting for coffees in the absence of running.

Rosy told me that she felt worried about us going to Costa Rica. I reassured her that I would keep in touch a lot and take care of myself. Anadi's business partner, asked me to work with him, as a client. Everything was shifting and changing, opening and expanding.

Day 158: Wednesday 16th October: *It echoed my experience of being with him*

We left Eastbourne at 3.15pm and drove to Hampshire to see Ros, for my monthly appointment. I had asked Anadi if he would come and do a session together. Ros had asked that we came with some clarity of an agenda, so that she could help us make the time really useful, and I'd told her that I'd like to explore my 'pulling away'.

We arrived not knowing what to expect – both Anadi and I were open to whatever emerged. The moment we arrived it felt good, and the time went so fast. We explored how with change comes loss and gain. Rather than the feelings I had of having lost myself, I saw how much I had gained. I might have lost some habits, but I had also gained so much new experience on levels that were beyond explanation.

Anadi and I both talked about the ways we live now, the changes within us, the re-writing of our narratives. We resolved to keep the connection always safe, and that way we would be able to keep ourselves safe within the relationship. So, the next time I feel the pulling away feeling, I could discuss the fear, rather than doing a speech about not being able to do relationship, which only ever served to make both of us feel unsafe.

I learned how much I used to pull away from my Dad and his control, while at the same time craving his approval. Of course, I was doing the same thing now – projecting onto Anadi, who didn't control in any way and approved all the time.

My coach, Tim, gave me lots of attention and it was so painful. So my relationship with men had essentially been a painful repeat of these patterns, until now, other than right at the beginning, in my first teenage love with Richard. I had come full circle and, after all the searching, had found what I had at the beginning, but with greater appreciation, wisdom, experience and understanding, and deeper love and connection than I ever knew possible. I had hoped and dreamed it was possible, but had in recent years given up looking, and so had Anadi. But we found one another, and now I was ready to write a new narrative. It became evident that I pulled away at points of deepening commitment; so in future, when I felt fear, we could talk about it and understand where the other was coming from.

Ros suggested that we had a conversation about what was unique about our connection, and what creativity we could explore emerging from it, especially as we set off on our adventures together. She asked Anadi what gifts he received being with me. He said that he was met on every level, that he was seen, that he could talk to me about everything and that he was understood.

Listening to him speak about his love for me and what he experienced in relationship, I was aware of something relaxing within me. I heard what he said and received it, perhaps because it was said in public, almost like a marriage ceremony. I felt like it echoed my experience of being with him.

I was also aware of the part of me that didn't quite trust. I cried at something Ros said because it accessed where I was afraid, where I was watchful, and it was evident that this was the seed of the place where I pull away when the fear got too much. I cried again when I said that I didn't really know if I could ever do 'this'.

'This?' queried Ros.

'Have a relationship like this,' I said. 'Because I've been so hurt.'

We left Ros feeling good, and so glad that we had gone to the session together. We talked all the way home and then decided to eat out before going home to bed.

Day 159: Thursday 17th October. *More space for others and for experiencing life, more capacity for fun*

This morning, the alarm went off, heralding an hour of email writing before a gentle run to ease my body back after the weeks of neural pain. My treatment with Greg on Tuesday had helped me so much: the pain was less, the range of movement more.

Anadi lay on top of me all warm and sleepy, a good morning hug before I slipped away to my computer. We started kissing and then in a tangled sleepy sensuous embrace he slipped inside me and we were making morning love, starting the day in praise of our love and deep connection and cementing further the depths we had reached in our session with Ros the previous evening.

Later when Anadi and I talked about how delicious our lovemaking was, he said to me, 'I was half asleep...' And in truth so was I. The sex felt so connected, so tantric and intimate: making love, becoming one, while honouring our separateness within the deepening of our love and connection.

I realised it was Day 160 of my being a girlfriend for a year and once again a full moon. Our symbol on the rock in Santorini would have the light of the full moon shining on it, deepening even further our commitment to the life we had created of love and consciousness.

In the evening, I went to Portsmouth with my friend, Wends, who I met at nursery school when we were four years old. We were lying, rather tipsily, on our hotel beds, having been out drinking cocktails and eating delicious food, when we realised that we were celebrating fifty years of friendship, under a full moon.

She texted her eldest daughter Ellie and mentioned our fifty year celebrations.

'Fifty years of what?' Ellie enquired. It transpired she didn't realise Wends and I were together...

'Fifty years since we met and of our friendship' Wends replied.

'Oh! You're with Ju...'

Wends and I hadn't seen one another on our own since March, when Anadi and I were right in the middle of our 'process'. Wends had said then: 'I feel good about this guy.' She said tonight: 'I really, really like him. He's so deep. And you're different,' she continued, 'without any tension at all, it seems.'

There *had* been an absence of tension. I felt so different that I no longer recognised myself; I didn't even try to remember 'who I was' now. My old skin had been shed and in its place was the new, the transformed, the released, the relaxed – no tension at all, it seemed. As each layer shed, I found myself letting go of old ways of being. Tried and tested ways had been surrendered and in their place was more fun, less rigidity, more spontaneity.

I remembered my mother's advice to me all those years ago before she died and left me at 16, with her words echoing around but not truly landing in my being: 'Darling, have fun...' I had always had energy and laughter in my life, I'd had relationship and experience and lived life to the full – but true, deep-down fun? That had eluded me, until now.

I could finally hear my mother's words loud and clear and feel them within my being. I had been having a lot of fun. Without the pressure of competition in my running, I felt more able to embrace the moment than ever before. And without competition? I liked the person I now saw mirrored. She was more at ease, looser, more relaxed. There was more room, even more space for others and for experiencing life, more capacity for fun.

Day 166: Thursday 24th October: *I resolved not to push, and he resolved to work on his adaptation*

A week had passed since I last wrote about being a girlfriend for a year; a week that passed in a blur of work for Anadi and I. In between work, we found the time to have an on-going dialogue about how we communicate the truth of who we are. The commitment to deepening in relationship asked that we shared our 'stuff' as it arose between us, rather than being reactive – or withdrawing to process it alone.

On Wednesday Anadi came home late from London and we talked late into the night, waking up on Thursday feeling very tired. It had been an ingrained and useful adaptation for Anadi to process alone and for me this touched the pain I experienced as a child of my Dad's withdrawal. I could see that Anadi's intention was to keep himself safe, from the wrath of *his* Dad's words and once again we saw how the complementary adaptations we had to our fathers meant that we had the opportunity to really shift this and to be truly close, truly connected.

Thursday felt hard. Although I was fully connected in all my sessions with my clients, nonetheless, the day passed with part of me longing to be with Anadi. That night, he said that he really saw how he avoided sharing with me, and how this separated us, and if anything, meant he experienced the feelings of 'being wrong' when all he was trying to do was the 'right thing': it can be so painful when we do the wrong thing for the right reason; confusing and painful.

In the midst of 'working it all out', Anadi said, 'I have never tried so hard in a relationship and never felt like I'm getting it so wrong'.

I said, 'All I have ever wanted is for someone to be really truthful about what is going on for them and I have never experienced it until now'.

So I resolved not to push, and he resolved to work on his adaptation.

Day 167: Friday 25th October: *Something profound had happened in our relating*

By Friday evening, we were sitting drinking cocktails in The Loft Bar in Eastbourne, and something profound had happened in our relating. Our shifts and deepening connection meant that I had, in many ways, forgotten who I was: the changes within and also in the outer realms of my life meant that I no longer expected to 'be in control of my life'. I was simply committed to love, to being truthful in every moment and to honouring the relating by speaking out.

Anadi's business partner's mum, and I had agreed to buy 5% each of his company's shares, after he and his partner had reached the end of the road with the third party we'd talked about on our holiday. The agreement was finalised last week, reflecting another deepening of a commitment to myself - in that I was risking being part of something, but also leaping without a safety net and trusting that one would appear. By spending my money on both our adventure and on shares in Anadi's venture – the venture that on the first day I met him I said would make him a lot of money - I 'put my money where my mouth is.'

In my own business I had never been so busy, never had so many souls finding their way to my door. There seemed to be no say for me in this, and so I started thinking that I needed to find

186

my inner voice, to have some say, to create the time to be, the time to contemplate and be with myself.

I had not been alone all year. I had not written or run as much as I would have liked – and yet what I had been doing I had liked. I was riding the wave, I was not falling off. It was powerful and huge and felt so right. I said to my friend Steph back in August that this year was going to continue to be busy, that sleep would be less than ever before, and that the pace would not lessen. I saw this and I was accurate in what I saw – and in the future?

In the future I intended to create more space for running and writing, while always opening to the souls that chose to cross my path, asking for the space to find their way home to themselves and so to their true direction out in the world and in relationship with others.

We came home high on two cocktails each, as well as the feeling of liberation that the promise of two days ahead, exclusively together, gave us. We talked, relaxed and reviewed the events of a very full week; a very creative productive full week for our businesses, but within that a deepening of our relating and of our love for one another.

We were lying up in our tree house after dinner, chatting and relaxing. Anadi started to stroke my pussy and gently, gradually we made love – amazing, sexy, passionate love. It was late and we were happy and relaxed and together. Sex kept getting better! And sex had always been good together. I had dreamed of this, a relationship that got deeper with sex got sexier and it was happening. I was living my dream.

Day 168: Saturday 26th October. *I knew the destruction, both mental and physical, of carrying on with a broken body*

On Saturday morning we woke up late. It was already 9.20am and the runners running Beachy Head were 20 minutes into their run. After some coffee and chatting and stretching, we headed off at 10.30 to run to watch the marathon, my hip only just healed enough to enjoy the nine miles we covered watching the runners run home. The day was clear and warm; I ran in shorts and a crop top. We stopped and had a chat with Ant Bliss, the photographer, who positioned himself at the top of the second to last hill, a mile from home. We spoke once a year at this spot! He was wrapped up against a strong wind. The leaders appeared, looking fresh – of course – the winners often do. We ran to Birling Gap but there was no sign of Greg or Rob. Something was amiss.

Rob eventually appeared looking very unhappy and without energy, slower than he had run the Beachy Head marathon in many years, blood streaked down his thigh – from running through brambles we found out later – and a general sadness in his being.

Greg didn't appear. He had been nursing a calf injury going into the race and after Rob had passed by I said to Anadi, 'I hope Greg has pulled out'. I knew the destruction, both mental and physical, of carrying on with a broken body. We ran to Birling Gap and as we were deciding where to go next, Jim ran past. He looked good and perfectly within his running.

In the pub afterwards we heard the tales, mainly of woe! Neither Anadi nor I felt we should have been running the race. The afternoon was a good one, friends gathering, a big crowd, lovely food, good beer. But Rob was very sad, he had just heard that his father was close to death. 'Nil by mouth' had been instructed and his hours were numbered. We didn't have a chance to really talk, as he joined in the party. His Dad passed away later that day. It was Miriam's birthday too – Rob's wife. Her comment on the marathon she had just run, when asked if she would do it again: 'No – I hated it!' She added, 'and it's my birthday, too!'

Day 169: Sunday 27th October. *Love expressed through the body, deeply and magnificently*

Anadi and I had a totally perfect day. We didn't get out of bed until 2.30pm – 3.30pm 'old time'. The clocks had gone back by an hour and we savoured that extra hour all day. Something had shifted within our relating. The last process we had been going through, the deepening of my request that Anadi shared himself and what was going on within him as it was happening; had been really and truly heard and a healing seemed to have occurred. I found myself speaking out and not feeling wrong, and Anadi was truly hearing me and not feeling wrong.

We were becoming closer; our love making even deeper, more relaxed, more connected, sexier than ever. 'is this possible?' I wondered. Sex with Anadi was better than I had ever experienced, and yet still we were going to new places all the time, a deepening of the intimacy and connection: love expressed through the body, deeply and magnificently.

I felt over the weekend that my love for Anadi was deeper than ever. I truly saw the child within him that had got hurt all that time ago, and yet I also saw before me the man, who shone bright and strong. Some shift had occurred which I could not explain, but I certainly felt it. We had a magical weekend, so magical that I once again experienced the feeling of never wanting the time to end, of time running out, of our time together being too short.

189

Day 175: Sat 2nd November. *I am loving the shift in our lovemaking*

On October 31st – Day 173 of being a girlfriend for a year – I bought 5% of Anadi's company. It felt like a chi shift, that a magic spell had been cast. On Tuesday night, he took me out and we ate tuna steak salad; on Wednesday night we went and drank a cocktail each and talked and talked. On Thursday we celebrated my buying the shares and made very sexy love again. I was loving the shift in our lovemaking. My previous experience of long-term relationship has been a dwindling of sex, or at the very least a dwindling of my or my partner's, or our mutual enthusiasm for sex. With Anadi I liked nothing more than lying naked with him, talking, cuddling, making out and making love.

Day 181: Friday 8th November: *Running to learn and learning to love*

This week was so busy, I woke up every morning tired, looking forward already to bed, not truly wanting to live the day ahead. I have always said that when this happens I must not work. I owe it to my clients not to work when I don't really want to. Each session I engaged in however, I loved: enriching, uplifting, the privilege of working alongside others so that they could become free too. But still I knew it was too much.

Today, I worked with Anadi and his partner. it was fun, I could see the company wanted to fly free too; to open cities to work smoothly, for the people within to be freer, more supported, and for life to be easier. The irony was that Anadi and I wanted none of this, we did not seek ease and being looked after. But we did seek increased depths of communication, and his software did enable this, ease of dialogue, connecting information, many people and even whole buildings talking and comparing notes. 'Are you too hot my dear? Or a little chilly perhaps?'

Later that day, Anadi and I drove to London, arriving quite late, around 9pm. We went straight to his local Indian restaurant and enjoyed really delicious food: a lovely evening, but I was tired from too much work. It was time to change, I knew this. Fear of money draining away – so fear itself – had kept me locked in with a lot of work. I needed this time though, and I liked seeing that I could earn a lot of money. But I did not want to rely on my clients. I wanted freedom.

In the night Anadi and I woke up and talked. Relationship and running were where I still felt my life's work lay. Running to learn and learning to love: this was all there was for me. Love was the theme in both. If I was truly resting in love and consciousness then my running would flow from the place Anadi and I had created: 'a life of love and consciousness and we are totally supported in this.'

Commitment to this path, of course, meant truly listening to our inner voices at all times. It made more 'conventional sense' to stay committed to making money, but it made more sense to my spirit to be free to love and run – and sleep more and make love with my twin flame.

Day 182: Saturday 9th November. *We had such a lot of fun – I was so glad I had decided to be a girlfriend for a year*

After my middle-of-the-night half-asleep chat with Anadi, I knew I must engage with my running once again, as this year my running path had slipped away. Indeed, only a month ago, I had 'let go' of competing, but on reflection it was not the competition I wanted to be free of. When I was a teenager, I wanted freedom from the pressure to win from my Dad and my coach, and all that this brought. That is what I wished to be free from. I wished to run free. And now I was, and I did run free.

So I was ready, having put my bags down, to take them up again and continue on this earthly journey, but with less baggage than before. I would only know how much I still carried as I journeyed and felt its weight. Maybe I was travelling truly light now. As Anadi and I let go of our possessions and life as we knew it, we would find out what held us down, what we still needed to clear from our being.

We woke up on Saturday morning and my waking thought was that I would run ultras, as I planned five years ago – in my fifties! Anadi lay on top of me and we looked into each other.

I want to be inside you,' he said, and we made love, so deeply, so connected – really amazing sex. I loved starting my day this way.

Andy texted to say he wouldn't be running in Trent Park, as we had assumed: it was his wife Helen's birthday and they were going into town for brunch.

'London town?' I asked Anadi.

'Yes.' he said.

'Can we go into town for brunch?' I asked.

'Of course we can,' he said.

We ran first, in Trent Park, muddy now – the dry summer paths transformed by autumn leaves and made wetter as the rain started to fall. And my Nike Frees had no grip! But I loved the run, my hip felt free and I was running without pain again.

We came back to Anadi's flat – now clean and ready for its new owners. We ran a bath and soaked together, then headed into town, I wanted to go to Covent Garden to the Crusting Pipe. I love listening to the classical buskers there.

We arrived to a chilly, Christmassy Covent Garden, the shops all shiny and sparkly. We made our way past the still, golden statue man, the clockwork silver man, and a man doing something with orange juice; into the esplanade and down the steps. A couple were just finishing and we took the baton from them for a table right under the Christmas tree, a giant of a tree reaching skyward up towards the roof where big red shiny baubles were suspended, the silver strobe directly in front of us sending light darting around the building.

We sat close together, the cold air turning my nose red. We drank coffee while listening to a man in a white T-shirt and jeans singing opera songs beautifully, and ordered a delicious lunch to share – pear and Stilton salad and a mezze platter. Everything tasted so good.

The door to which only the performers have the key was open; folk were gathering to make up a string quintet – three violins, a viola and a cello. The performers, two women and three men, were also casually dressed. They warmed up a bit and proceeded to play uplifting classical music with energy, joy and enthusiasm. I didn't want them to stop.

Finishing our meal with dessert and steaming coffee we decided it was time to move, to get the chill out of our bodies, to walk through the lively streets before winding our way back to Enfield. It was a really lovely, happy day together. I totally loved being with Anadi, wherever we were and whatever we were doing. We had such a lot of fun – I was so glad I had decided to be a girlfriend for a year.

Day 183: Sunday 10th November. *I really like loving his family and them loving me!*

Anadi and I met Andy to run in Trent Park. It was a glorious morning. He ran a lap with us which gave Anadi a chance to talk business with him; Andy had contacts in IBM who could be helpful.

Anadi cooked us a delicious lunch before we set off on a day of visiting relatives. We had a cup of tea with his Dad, then his Gran. I had a really nice time. I really like loving his family and them loving me! We stopped off to see my Auntie Helen on the way home. It didn't look comfortable being in her body any more, but she seemed to be holding on for a reason: maybe she was determined to get to 100 years of being in a body on this planet. Who knows? But we stayed an hour, which passed easily. Anadi was easy to be with in that strange environment, too hot really, with the background noise of residents' televisions and bleeping call bells at different pitches. I showed him a picture of me aged 38 with my Auntie Helen. He said I look the same. I feel I do, really and truly, but I was younger in understanding and less clear then.

Day 184: Mon 11th November. *It seemed that I was on the running path once more*

I had taken to having a treatment with Greg (Funnell) on Monday mornings. I've known Greg for four years. We first met going through a gate on the Downs and the next time we met I asked him if he would be willing to record a podcast with me. He was willing, and in the interview Greg said how much Ultra Running called him. And so, last April, Anadi and I stood in the rain at Jevington waiting for Greg, who soon came bounding towards us with only about five or six miles to run in the South Downs 50. Greg might not have felt like he was bounding of course, but his energy looked buoyant, and he had weathered hail and rain and visibility of only two foot ahead. Of course there were patches where he felt 'tired', as he recounted later.

After seeing him round the corner to tackle the last hill to home, Anadi and I had driven to the sports park, arriving just in time to see him finish in seventh position – it seemed he had found his event. Watching Greg, I was reminded of running from London to Brighton in 2008, in the rain: a life-changing day, step after step all day long with the rain pouring down. I loved it and I decided I would 'become an Ultra Runner' in my fifties, which were beginning the following year.

In the April, one month before my 50th birthday, I ran 100k in Copenhagen. I was on a mini break with my oldest friend Wends, to celebrate our 50th birthdays.

'Would you mind if I spent the first day running?' I asked her. Luckily she didn't and equally luckily it was a beautiful spring day, warm and sunny, and the course traversed ten times around a beautiful lake. My mantra for the entire race – while I could still articulate it in my head – was, 'They will soar on wings like eagles; they will run and not grow weary' (Isaiah 40:31). It worked for me, keeping me in my rhythm and in the step.

I turned 50 that May, 2009, and I had not yet run another Ultra. My hip had been sore and challenged for a few weeks now, which brought me into Greg's treatment room again. His magical hands set me back on the running path and today, with the conversation turning once more to running destinations ahead, somehow the session ended with Greg sending me the link to enter the South Downs 50 miles on April 5th 2014. I had two six week blocks before the race: plenty of time to run and run and run, doing what I love to do, free as a bird, running mile after mile after mile. But was it a good idea to run this race? Was it wise, I asked myself? I found myself answering that it was what I came to the planet to do, to run and become all I know, all I am and all I know deep inside.

Of course this is only the I am I think I am, which is not. There is no 'I' in truth, and 'I' run because running knows this – spirit free – expressing consciousness and love and light through the body, in the run, in the step, in the moment, staying still within to run and become free.

'They will soar on wings like eagles; they will run and not grow weary.'

It seemed that I was on the running path once more.

Day 185: Tuesday 12th November. *Anadi was becoming enthused at the thought of training with me*

Anadi and I started our day with ten miles in the rain. It was a wonderful way to start the day. Anadi was becoming enthused at the thought of training with me on some of my long efforts. 'I'm up for doing some 20 mile runs' he said. I decided I'd remind him of this when we were snuggled up in bed in January and February.

Day 186: Wednesday 13th November. *Now, with Anadi, everything was different*

On Wednesday morning I met my friend Lawrence for a coffee. He was writing a book and as a way of an introduction he wrote down the three things that made him happy: his children smiling, someone saying they love him, and running. He said he wasn't doing enough running. I told him I had entered the 50 miler. He told me he had resolved to run more next year, so I hoped we could meet again on the run.

I was having a 'play day'. After meeting Lawrence, I drove to Lewes to take Ange out for her belated birthday lunch. Her birthday is in May! We had a lovely time. She laughed when I told her of my plan to run the South Downs 50 – especially as only two weeks ago I had announced my retirement from competition. But she said that although I could help people every hour of the day, she thought it would be good for my soul to be on the running trail again, as well as heading out with Anadi to adventure together.

I then drove to Ros and explored with her the wound that was still healing: the wound that felt unsafe, that all the good would come tumbling down, that it would end and I would be left because I am essentially wrong, bad and flawed and I must 'earn' my place on this planet.

Of course, I knew this was not true: my conscious adult self knew this, and most of the time I was not in touch with this wounded place because it was so much more healed than ever before. But meeting Anadi, setting off on this adventure with him and the idea of leaping into love still touched this place of such vulnerability - especially as parts of the story seemed to be repeating. Once again I was with a man who was striving for a dream to come true, a dream not yet realised, for which he had sacrificed much and put everything into. The old story ran that I was of less importance – that my role was to encourage and support and then when the man was flying I would be left with learning but not with the love I longed and yearned for.

Now, with Anadi, everything was different. The fear still arose, but I was able to release it and by doing so I was set free. I was free to know that we were at the centre of one another's world, because we were one, but within that trust and surrender arose the freedom to be ourselves, even more powerfully.

Kahlil Gibran's poem, *On Love*, had always spoken to me and now I was living it: *Even as he ascends to your height and caresses your tenderest branches that quiver in the sun, So shall he descend to your roots and shake them in their clinging to the earth ... Think not you can direct the course of love, for love, if it finds you worthy, directs your course.*

Anadi had gone to London for a big day of presentations at a conference. He sent me a picture of his business's stand, which looked great. As the day unfolded, he reported on the success of their presentations and the enthusiasm for their software. He had recently put in a facility to track underground pipes. I particularly liked this function, which looked amazing: multi-coloured, which of course may be a reason it spoke to me.

Day 191: Monday 18th November. *My body was once more 'mine'*

Anadi and I spent the weekend having a break in Dorset. On Friday night we travelled to Eype, where Amy had orchestrated another amazing experience for us. The journey was easy. Even with Friday night traffic, we stopped on the M27 for coffee and arrived in Eype at 8.27pm with a sign at the entrance saying food was served in the evening until 8.30pm. Our friendly inn-keeper assured us that they wouldn't have let us go hungry and brought us delicious lasagne, with salad and garlic bread, chips and beer. It was delicious and very welcome, though I realised Anadi and I were both unrecognisable in some of the food choices we were now making. We were sharing the dining area with a couple from Scotland who looked like they had been walking the coastal path all day, and were relaxing, playing cards and drinking wine.

Our room had a lovely four poster bed and we were glad to fall into it and into each other. We were entwined with each other energetically, in the centre point of the timelessness we had become familiar with in our lives together, in which time ceased to exist and yet hours passed and we didn't know how it had happened. It was like being transported. Something in me opened at the point of orgasm, energy coursed through my legs and my body felt very sensitive, too sensitive to touch. I felt spaced out, which went on for hours; meaning that post-sex snuggling felt too much and I was also very hot. I managed to sleep fitfully, but I kept waking, my body still coursing with energy and my legs feeling particularly 'jumpy'! Eventually in the early hours of the morning it settled and I could cuddle in with Anadi again, and be touched. My body was once more 'mine'.

The next morning we woke to a beautiful view of the Dorset coastline. Running up the steep grassy slope later, I recalled the times 30 and even 40 years ago that I ran along these same cliffs, and even earlier than that walked up to Golden Cap, just a few hills away from us. There wasn't time for us to run to and get back for breakfast, but there rising silently up from the sea shore, its magnificence was just as I remembered when Rosy and I strode up there with my Dad, aged only 10 and 8 and then rolled down the slopes on our sides in peals of laughter and abandonment.

Breakfast was a wonderful affair, both in terms of our relating and the amazing food – smoked salmon and scrambled egg for me, with fruit salad and coffee with cream; a fry-up for Anadi. We then we drove on to Lyme to see Rosy and her family. Spending time together as a family was special, and watching Anadi on the beach throwing stones with Jess as the light faded was beautiful, Rosy and I watching and chatting together on the sea wall.

We returned home and Jamie and Anadi played guitar together while Rosy, Jess, Nick and I chatted and readied ourselves for 'Strictly Come Dancing', their regular Saturday night routine. Anadi pointed out that this was the first time we had watched TV in all the time we had been together.

When I returned home on Monday morning, I did more clearing, then went to the tip and to the charity shop. The flat was feeling different. The energy was clearer and lighter again.

I could not wait for our new life to begin, My spirit was champing at the bit and I felt that I was free.

Day 192: Tuesday 21st November. *The pain had come up to be healed*

Amy and I spent the morning clearing and she took the kitchen table, two chairs and the wicker chair to bits – furniture she put together seven years ago – then we went to the tip together, freeing me further from possessions and the weight of stuff.

Later, Anadi and I talked about the possibility of a power struggle between us and the pain that would come with this. We had both been wounded as children by not being celebrated for our sparks of light. In fact the reverse happened and we were contained. I had internalised that I was wrong, and Anadi had been verbally crushed.

I sometimes saw my deeply symbiotic core wound start to ooze and open when Anadi and I were parted, sometimes even only for a day, as his brilliance started to shine separate from me and it touched in me the past wounding of not being allowed to shine myself.

I knew that if it was triggered in any way then the pain had come up to be healed, and in this relationship with Anadi, this was exactly what was occurring. In his shining new venture and his courage and his world opening, I often saw reflected there the fear of my own limitations and this caused distress.

Day 193: Wednesday 20th November. *I felt only my certainty, my confidence, and the joy of my own expression*

This morning as Anadi and I sat together, with me drinking my second cup of coffee (having decided not to brave the elements – pouring rain and wind on a cold November day!) I shared with him how his journey was accessing the part of me that wanted to soar to great heights, to be seen and recognised and succeed to the highest level. I explained that it brought this up in me, and I

200

then found myself feeling conflicted, and deemed my feelings 'uncharitable' (to be thinking about me, me, me!) and 'unspiritual' (to be concerned and attached to an earthly ego desire for self actualisation).

Yet by the end of the day, travelling back on the train after working in London, I felt good. I had watched the effect of my work all day and something within me shifted. I felt prepared to engage fully with my gift, to own its power, to give myself permission to use my emotional radar and allow in the information that I received about others. I opened to accepting this, whether I was 'in my room' and 'officially working' or whether I was 'out and about'. This freed me.

I did not need to let Anadi know that I saw my gifts clearly, because he saw it clearly too. He knew that I knew what I was able to give to others through my work here on earth and the gifts I had within me. After today's experiences, I felt only my certainty, my confidence, and the joy of my own expression.

Day 194: Thursday 21st November. *We saw how much healing was happening*

Today, Anadi and I did go for a run – despite the rain and wind. Before we left, we sat drinking tea and coffee on the floor in our empty kitchen that now echoed a bit, enjoying our warm drinks before heading out onto the chilly seafront.

As we ran, I shared with him that, when he told me about showing his software to others and how impressed they were, I sometimes had to 'work' with the bit that was wounded; the part that was 'not allowed' to celebrate my own achievements that others might be impressed by, long since disowned. Now, I felt that this was healing within me through my noticing it pass through. I shared with him how I had been reflecting on this the previous day.

He told me that when he told people what he had been doing, there was something in him truly recognising himself and his talents and what he had created. He spoke of how he was not seen when he was younger, and his abilities and spark, far from recognised, were in fact crushed.

We saw how we were healing together, and how the shared wounds could create difficulty within our relating. Imagine if every time he shared with pride his achievements, this touched my wound, the place where my achievements had not been celebrated. This could create all manner of difficulties. Instead, we explored our childhood together as we ran in the rain. We saw how much healing was happening and how we were giving ourselves and one another the chance to shine with all the light that is within us.

Day 200: Wednesday 27th November. *It was the beginning of us being of 'no fixed abode'*

I spent the morning with Amy, creating Skype and email packages for coaching. Last night Anadi created a Google booking system, connecting it to PayPal and then to my site. I was on the move and the movement was allowing me to be *more* accessible rather than less accessible.

Fi called me, very upset because there had been much drama with 'the room'. The time that the toilet was taking was the problem, the builders spending lots of time 'sucking their teeth'. Fi said she felt surrounded by 'pessimistic men'. Today was the day I had been supposed to move in to the new room. Fi had let me know on Monday that this wouldn't be possible, and Amy had been able to get us 'squeezed in' with the removal people for a move on Monday 2nd December. It transpired today that the room/toilet would still be in the 'creative process' then. I was glad to be able to sit in my empty kitchen and write about being girlfriend for a year.

Last weekend passed in a blur: a happy one, but non-stop work and socialising. Every day until we left had been filled with something. Perhaps my life would always be full. I lived in relationship, essentially with myself, but the deeper I went into connection with me, the deeper it seemed I was in connection with others and particularly with Anadi.

I felt energised and excited. I was looking forward to our trip, feeling very excited because it was more than a trip. It was the beginning of us being of 'no fixed abode'.

Day 201: Thursday 28th November. *We were doing it anyway and trusting*

Yesterday, more progress was made with my room. The days were flying by! Last weekend, Anadi's old friends Kamran and Sherry came to stay and we all went to see *Fiddler on the Roof*. 'Starsky' (Paul Michael Glaser) from Starsky and Hutch played the lead role as Tevye. It was wonderful to see him on stage, still doing his thing, aged 70.

Anadi and I had been talking in the week about freedom being about enjoying our creativity, allowing its flow – and on stage in front of us, was someone doing exactly that, forty years on from the time that watching him on Saturday night TV was part of our fabric of growing up.

Anadi had so much opening up with his business and I had so many clients to respond to. Anadi said yesterday that he was glad to be building his businesses while we were setting ourselves free to live a nomadic lifestyle. Rather than saying we will 'do it in five years when we have made the money', we were doing it anyway and trusting that following our hearts, listening to our inner voice, and being committed to a life of love and consciousness meaning that we would be supported in our every move. We had taken the red pill (as in *The Matrix*) and there was no going back.

Yesterday Amy and I 'got organised', amid the slight chaos of a not ready room for me to move into. We printed off all our documents ready for us to catch the 4.30pm train to London on Friday week. She was going to print off our boarding passes on that Friday morning and meet us at the station with them, then wave us off on our adventure…

Day 204: Sunday 1st December. *We had six days until we headed off on our nomadic adventure*

We ran 16 miles on the downs this morning with Rob and Rupert. It was a fabulous run. The air was still and clear, the downs were quite dry underfoot and the four of us ran and chatted like old friends, as if we ran together every Sunday. We *are* old friends, and Anadi had been welcomed into the group, but it was only the second time this year that I had attended a Sunday morning long run – this year's Sunday mornings have mainly been spent in bed!

For the past few years, every Sunday would see me rising at 6am to meet 'the boys' at 7am. We had trained together for ultras and marathons, and met up just to go running, connect and talk. I had been circling the downs with Rob for 13 years. He was now in training for the South Downs 100 miles in July and I was in training for the South Downs 50 miles in April so our running paths were converging once again as we prepared to put in the miles that would ensure we could run and run across the Downs we know so well in our ultra challenges.

Today was my first long run since I was injured 10 weeks ago; my first steps towards being fit enough to run for 50 miles from Worthing to Eastbourne. We had six days until we headed off on our nomadic adventure.

I had been back in the gym with Matt. All year long, I'd been saying how much I would like to do twice a week conditioning training, but it never quite fitted until now. However, I knew it would. When we 'put it out there', when we commit to a course, we will find that things conspire to lead us to that destination and we start doing things that naturally lead us there.

The secret I learned a long time ago (the hard way!) is that there is no rush. Things happen in their own time. I learned this in my work long before I learned it in my own life. I instinctively knew that I must stay on the shoulder of my clients, not rush ahead – that my work was simply to be there to guide and support. Which way they went and how much time it took was their job. Mine was simply 'to feed and water the plant'. It took a little longer to apply this in my own life and I crashed and burned many times before settling more easily into the moment and going with the flow.

After my hip injury kicked in, it made me readdress giving time to balancing and flexibility work on a daily basis. It also meant I didn't go in the gym for a few weeks. Anadi and I were flying to Costa Rica on 6th December, and I had five sessions left in a block I'd booked with Matt. To use them up, I was in the gym twice last week and twice again this week. So it had happened, and I'd already started to feel the benefit: my running was balanced and my left side was feeling strong. As I was once again heading towards a 50 mile journey across the downs in April, balance and strength, as well as endurance, were necessary ingredients for me to focus on.

The chi of running is key – if my hip is out it is hard to run five miles, let alone 50. Running is a natural movement, but it also shows us, within each step, where we are unbalanced – where we need to listen to our bodies. I was listening to mine.

Day 205: Monday 2nd December. *My life with Anadi had been magical so far*

I was sitting on the floor in my empty kitchen, with a coffee in front of me and my therapy room all packed up. I'd had an amazing weekend. Indeed, my life with Anadi had been magical so far. Being with him was a joy every day.

The first morning that we woke up together, I'd told him that I had always hoped to be in a relationship where the other would be as willing as me to explore intimacy, deeply, with no limits, to share and grow together, but also to be free. And now we were living this.

Freedom is vital for me, and I have felt always that freedom, love and consciousness are the same – together, like a holy trinity. True love frees the other: to be all that they can be; to support their process; to encourage them to grow and to dare to grow too; to face anything that arises within the relating; to be prepared to be completely vulnerable and open to becoming whole through exposing feelings and processes to each other.

Anadi had met me here and as we shed our belongings, I felt a real sense of us taking one another by the hand and leaping into the void, into the future, into infinite love.

Day 203: Saturday 30ᵗʰ November. *His nomadic lifestyle choice wasn't an issue for the company*

This morning, Anadi's business partner called him to say that a company had offered £5 million shares and a £120,000 pay packet apiece to acquire their company and employ them as department heads. The negotiations had been on-going for a few weeks and the company concerned had one a multi-billion pound deal to build a 'future city' in Brazil. This meant Anadi could be working in Brazil part time. His nomadic lifestyle choice wasn't an issue for the company - which is just as well because that is how Anadi now worked!

Day 205: Monday 2nd November. *The symmetry felt good*

The removal men arrived today: the same pair who had moved me from my previous flat! The symmetry felt good. Amy and I sat in her car watching my belongings go down the road in a van and out of sight.

I spent the day getting my new therapy room ready and saw some clients. I enjoyed seeing them all, but I also had to 'dig in', and was initially aware of the feeling of looking forward to the end. I was feeling challenged to live in the moment, though once with a client I was totally there

Anadi picked me up at 9pm and we ate leftover tuna bake upstairs in our 'treehouse'.

Day 206: Tuesday 3rd November. *I was living as I foresaw and even went into therapy to explore*

Today, we ran round the Hollow and Anadi and I spoke about how important it was to live these last days fully before we headed out on our life of freedom and 'No Fixed Abode'. In the evening, we caught the 5.04pm train to Brighton and walked through the chilly streets to Si's wine bar, 'Ten Green Bottles'. It was warm and bright inside, full of the buzz of 'relaxing over a glass of wine after work' energy. A wine tasting with a group from American Express occupied the middle table and Anadi and I settled in on one of the tables at the side.

My friend Debs arrived after half an hour with an envelope of money for me. She had booked eight sessions with me for her brother, as his Christmas present. We had a quick catch up for half an hour and decided that we were finally ready to have the lunch in the Oxo Tower we had been planning for twenty years, to mark that we were living our dream. We decided that time was now. Debs had just won her biggest contract to date and I was living as I foresaw and even went into therapy to explore: how to live a spiritual life while experiencing being a top level businesswoman in a top level relationship and competing at top level in my sport.

We made our way to a nearby restaurant to meet my brother Stuart, his wife Sue, my niece Kelly and her boyfriend Kristen. It was a good evening. He, Sue and Anadi connected and got on well, there was much laughter and animated conversation, the food was delicious and the evening was a great success.

Day 209: Friday 6th December. *Friday – our leaving day - was upon us!*

Friday – our leaving day – was upon us! We made our way through Eastbourne with our bags on our shoulders to meet Amy at the station for a hot chocolate, a goodbye hug and the delivery of our boarding passes before climbing aboard the 16.31 train to London. As the train pulled out we remembered that part of the 'meeting at the station mission' had been to hand over our keys to Amy, so that she could organise final clearing and cleaning before handing the flat and keys back to my landlord. But the keys were still in our bags!

We emerged into the franticness of Friday night rush hour at Waterloo, abandoned our bags at left luggage, bought a Jiffy bag and some stamps to send our keys back to Eastbourne, then made our way to the Young Vic Theatre where our friend Jonny was performing in 'Beauty and the Beast'. This was our only chance to see it.

The show depicted the true story of the love affair between a beauty queen called Julie, and her partner, Mat. Mat's mother was one of the many women encouraged to take the drug called Thalidomide, ostensibly to cure morning sickness with no ill effect to mother or child. As we are now fully aware, there was great cost to child and to mother. I really loved the show: it made me want to press 'rewind' and watch it all over again, straight away. We then had a drink and a quick catch up with Jonny in the bar, as we were on a reasonably tight schedule to collect our luggage before it was locked away for the night.

We arrived at our hotel at Heathrow and I had an urge for the dessert we'd had no time for earlier. We ordered chocolate cheesecake with macaroon biscuits and sat up in bed eating the most delicious creation imaginable at 1am.

The alarm going off less than four hours later was a little disorientating, but with the airport right next to the hotel, we found ourselves propelled through the process of dropping our bags and were sitting with cappuccino in front of us by 6am, as if by magic.

Day 210: Saturday 7th December. *It did feel hard at the time though*

When we got on the plane today, there was a hold-up. Trouble with the telephone system had affected air traffic control which meant a two hour delay. We were grateful for the four hour transfer time in Madrid before our flight to Costa Rica. The captain announced we'd arrive in Madrid at about 1pm rather than 10am – just in time for lunch.

When we arrived, the hills of Madrid spread around us in panoramic view from the airport windows. The adventures on our planet as our home, with No Fixed Abode, stretched in front of us. Though I'd had to endure some of last week, and be patient, in hindsight it seemed a dot of time. Even with the delay, the journey seemed swift.

We slept and ate, and slept and read, and drank water and slept some more. At one point we attempted to watch a film but it was in Spanish. It was only as we came near to landing we realised I had changed the channel to Spanish-speaking.

We emerged into the life and heat of San Jose airport at 8.30pm, though for our body clock it was 3.30am. I texted Rosy in the loo and she replied immediately, having woken up a minute before I texted her. Anadi went to fetch our bags from the baggage carousel and, while I waited, I checked my emails and noticed how many people had commented on the blog I'd posted at Madrid.

'Can we do that later?' Anadi said.

His tone of voice touched my stuff, and my checking of mails and not getting a move on touched his. Both of us had the same childhood wounding about following everyone else's agenda, and not ours, so the tiny incident was a touch paper to the same wound in us both. As we felt close, it was inevitable that 'stuff' would come up for healing - though this never feels nice at the time! So it came to pass that we emerged from San Jose airport into the street fighting one another. We were greeted by a throng of people and lines of taxi drivers all wanting our fare. It was all a blur as we continued to spit and spat at each other.

Eventually despite our 'cross energy' we managed to work out which transfer bus we needed, but not before I said I knew I was right about what I had picked up in his tone, and Anadi said, 'Of course you are' with another 'tone'. 'Fuck off' I responded. That ended it really, I knew I had gone too far, although Anadi didn't react at all to me saying 'Fuck off' – and so we made up. We worked out what had happened too.

This is what I found so incredible and enriching and healing about being with Anadi, apart from the fact that I loved him so deeply; he was always willing to work things through until we were clear. And, of course, this meant our love could deepen and expand without limits. It did feel hard at the time though.

We arrived at our hotel in San Jose, where we spent a night before travelling on to stay with Rickee, an old friend of Anadi's living out here. The hotel was lovely, with a king size bed and really friendly staff.

As it was only 9.30pm, we decided to have a bath together to wash away the 25 hours of travelling before going for a wander and getting some supper. We found a lively Mexican restaurant and were quite possibly saved from ourselves by our order for a Margarita cocktail not being possible as they has just opened and didn't yet have a liquor licence.

We had a delicious plate of nachos, ginger ale for me and Coke for Anadi, then went back to our king size bed at about midnight (6am for our bodies!) We made love, passionately and beautifully, deeply connected in the heat, our sweaty bodies surrendering to one another in glorious orgasmic bliss.

Day 211: Sunday 8th December. *There was a strange energy in it, of spirits long gone, or energies that were trying to say something*

In the morning, we were awake before 7am (our new time) and found our way to the gym. Half an hour on the treadmill unravelled the stiffness of our sitting for so long. Breakfast was delicious and the timing was perfect.

Our transfer bus arrived and we joined two Americans on their way to a forestry conservation retreat. About an hour down the road, we picked up a retired American husband and wife on an adventure holiday – a bit too adventurous for the woman, Sharon, but she told us she was glad she had experienced the fear of traversing high mountainous terrain – after the event.

We were dropped at the hotel, and I stayed with bags while Anadi went for a look around.

'Whoop, whoop!' I heard. Rickee and Anadi had found one another, and immediately started catching up on the seven years since they'd last seen each other, during Anadi's days as a musician.

Rickee said his apartment and ours were next door and, slinging our bags over our shoulders, we walked up the dirt track. Our apartment wasn't quite ready, as Rickee had got muddled with dates and was expecting us on Tuesday, but the couple in the apartment were happy to move to stay with Rickee until theirs was ready.

Rickee took us up the road for lunch where we sat until dark, drinking beer and eating delicious local food, his seven year old playing with us and entertaining himself with inexpensive toys while Rickee and Anadi caught up.

We walked home along the dirt track in the dark, the river beside us, full of crocodiles, with Rickee telling us a story about the day the white horses walked home with him to keep him safe from the crocodiles!

Anadi and I were shown to our apartment, which was beautiful. There was a strange energy in it, of spirits long gone, or energies that were trying to say something. I felt this particularly in the kitchen and back bedroom. Anadi and I fell into bed, and a deep, deep sleep.

Day 212: Monday 9th December. *We felt alive and free*

We rose early, with the jungle squawking around us. We ran to the beach, past the bars and the shops, alive, colourful, and rustic. It was a magical beach: a vast expanse of sand, with huge waves rolling in. The surfers dotted and scattered on the sea waiting for their next wave. We ran until we met the rocks. We clambered up a rocky path to the road, passing a man living on the beach – a westerner. He didn't want to engage, and he had a huge machete by his side.

We dropped back onto the beach and ran to the furthest point, where we sat on our heels watching majestic birds sweeping round above us. We turned for home and about halfway along the beach we dived into the ocean. Huge waves battered and swirled us. We felt alive and free.

Day 213: Tuesday 13th December. *The phrase 'Pura Vida' sprang to mind*

Sitting by the pool in Dominical, Costa Rica, with Anadi working beside me, the phrase *Pura Vida* sprang to mind: a Costa Rican expression that literally translates as 'pure life' but is more akin to 'full of life', 'this is living' or 'real living'.

Day 215: Thursday 12th December. *Each day the waves seem to be getting bigger*

Today, we ran right to the point again, and on the way five dogs bounded up to us, barking wildly and rather menacingly. We stopped and walked and their owner appeared from the woodland and called them back. We went to the furthest tip by walking over the rocks, then ran back along the beach to some jagged rocks which we clambered over and sat on top of, with the waves crashing against them, and little crabs scurrying everywhere.

We stopped at the end and dived into the sea, which is now the way we finish all our runs. Each day the waves seem to be getting bigger.

Day 216: Friday 13th December. *We had a real sense of living our life, rather than 'being on holiday'*

We woke to the sounds of the jungle at 5.30am: something we were already becoming used to. The air was alive and vibrant with noise, and the humidity hung in the air, as always. We sleep with a fan on, whirring above our bed, an old-fashioned contraption hanging from the light and circling slowly, but effectively moving the air, stopping us from dripping with sweat all night.

We had become accustomed to sweating all day, but thankfully the cooler night air and the wind from the fan meant we could sleep entwined together all night long, as we liked to do. At 5.30am we moved sleepily into morning lovemaking, kissing and caressing and then fucking with abandon. We were certainly sweating then!

Anadi told me, 'I feel like we are closer than ever, and I am more in love with you than ever! I was totally in love with you anyway, but it has deepened'. I echoed this and he wanted me to expand on my feelings:

'It's because you're sharing yourself more,' I said. 'It means I feel closer to you and safe.'

He smiled and replied, 'And I now know that you aren't going to go anywhere'.

We drank coffee on the step and looked at emails. I spoke for half an hour with a client. Another coffee by the pool with some chocolate, and then it was 8am and time for us to run. But my body was so tired... Instead, we decided to walk to the ocean and, taking our shoes and socks off, continued along the shoreline to a place that was deserted, where we shed our clothes and dived naked into the surf.

On our way home, we stopped at the supermarket for supplies before walking the last mile home beside the river full of the crocodiles we had not yet seen. We met Tim walking the other way with his dog Kai on a lead. Tim lived in a house on the land where our home (for three weeks!) was situated. He's a designer and a surfer and we had spoken to him the first couple of days we were here. We were offered his front room as an office, because otherwise we could only get the internet on their front step or by the pool: not so good either for Anadi's computer or for our bodies, hour after hour exposed to the powerful sun. The set-up allowed us to work, rest and play together. I had done two Skype sessions with clients already and was becoming totally at ease with the idea of working with people via technology all over the world, as well as face-to-face.

Tim's day had begun with the girlfriend of one of the tenants crying and shrieking at his door, calling out 'Jack, Jack' between her sobs. Tim had gone to the house above the bar that Jack rented, to find him dead. We spoke together about it for a while, and he was philosophical – 'It's where we're all heading' – but clearly shaken.

Our walk into town for food was along a stony path. Darkness fell quickly and like a velvet curtain between 5.30 and 6pm, which meant eating out at 7.30 felt far later than it was. We ate delicious fresh food in the Tortilla Flats restaurant, as we had the night before. The food tasted amazing, and we were so hungry. We were eating a lot of fresh pineapple in the day and not much else, other than protein recovery drink and coffee and chocolate, so our evening meal was very welcome.

We had a real sense of living our life, rather than 'being on holiday'. We were truly living as we liked to, working and playing and living together side by side.

Day 218: Sunday 15th December. *To fully live is to learn how to let go*

Today, we were swimming and got caught up in a current that was pulling us out to sea. It all happened in an instant. Everything was a blur as I panicked and cried and was swirled by the waves and swallowed water and coughed. I couldn't breathe until Anadi managed to drag me out. I had faced the void, faced death itself.

I have spent my life conscious of death. The family dog died the day my sister was born. My mother was at the hospital in labour when my father wrapped the little dachshund in a blanket. 'Where are you taking Judy?' I asked. 'To the vet,' he replied. I never saw her again…

My Grandmother died when I was six years old. She lived with us and had gone into hospital with pneumonia. I was aware she had died but had not been told, because my little sister was going into hospital to have her adenoids out and my parents did not want hospital to appear a scary place from which you might not return. 'When is Granny coming home?' I asked my mother, already knowing the answer.

My Grandpa was the next to leave his body, when I was eight. He had already taught me many valuable lessons about how to live, which I have carried with me to this day, so in truth he did not go anywhere: he has always been here with me.

At sixteen years old, I was visiting my very ill Mother in hospital on a Thursday afternoon, I had stopped in to see her after school. She needed oxygen to help her breathe. I kissed her goodbye as I was leaving, and I turned back, waved to her from the door and said 'See you at the weekend, Mummy'. I never saw her again.

So – a friend of death I became. I knew early in my life that I wanted to learn to embrace this ending that would come sometime to me, so that I might fully live now.

In the afternoon, Anadi and I lay on our bed with the doors to the balcony open. We lay there chatting and leaning against one another for over two hours watching day leave and night fall. It was a beautiful experience. Music started up in the hotel next door. The guy singing was singing songs we knew well and in the style of the original singer. We decided to go along and listen, so we wandered along to the hotel and sat by the pool under the nearly full moon, listening to the singer sing his songs until we were ready for supper and bed.

We had gone from 'the sublime to the ridiculous' – starting this year with bedtimes of 2am, 3am, 4am and even a 5am, but with night falling before 6pm here we seemed to have taken to being in bed before 9pm – and awake at 5.30am!

Day 219: Monday 16th December. *I let go of life itself and just relaxed and swam*

Even after a week of this lifestyle, Anadi and I were aware that this was just the beginning of a journey together where the planet quite literally was our home. 'The world is our oyster.' We had got into the habit of exercising on the balcony, after running, with a piece of training equipment that Matt had lent me. My body was strengthening, the left side catching up with the right and I was doing what I was born to do: running in the sun, free of pain and anxiety; running and running because running was what I came here to do. I learned through running and I learned through relationship.

Today, the sun was particularly bright and hot. Anadi and I worked in our office, having eaten fresh pineapple and brioche, drunk coffee, and prepared ourselves for the day.

When we went swimming, we tried to be wise, careful not to have a repeat of the day before, and had our feet on the floor of the ocean. The current still swirled us, unawares, and in an instant we were in more danger than before. I did not panic. I was afraid, but I accepted the fact that we were powerless against the power of the sea, that we could not fight the current and that it was dragging us out.

The current was pulling us out and across the sea, but with each wave that came, Anadi shouted to me: 'Swim, swim, use the wave to get you in'. So I did, and I remembered his face, his eyes still and calm, but concern in his being.

'We're in real danger,' I said to him 'Help me, please help me.'

'We are in danger,' he said. 'Swim.' He said again, 'swim'.

'I'm exhausted.' I said as a wave crashed on me and swirled me under. Once it was all over I took a huge gulp of air, and then it happened again.

I reached for Anadi and we briefly held hands before the side of a wave took him and tumbled him under and away from me. He looked so fragile. These waves were six foot high. We hadn't intended to go out so far.

'Swim, swim, keep swimming,' Anadi said again. I swam and I swam. I turned my head to the right.

'Please help me,' I said to the universe, to consciousness itself. And I relaxed and let go. Let go of everything I knew. I let go of life itself and just relaxed and swam.

My foot touched the ocean floor again. 'Dig in, dig in,' Anadi called. The current sucked us back again, but we had a foothold. He grabbed my hand and we pushed against the current, able to walk now. We were both breathing very hard. And then we were home and dry.

Anadi put his arm around me. I leaned against him, exhausted, breathing hard. He was panting too. We were utterly drained. I glanced up and saw a man standing on the beach, his hands on his hips watching us. It looked like he had been keeping an eye on the situation. There would have been no point him coming in to help. He would simply have endangered himself. But he had been watching.

We sat on the log, recovering. We had already run eight miles that day. We were so hungry. The run had been a profound one anyway, as we had been exploring letting go more deeply. We had let go of one another in the course of the past year, which is why we were so deeply connected. I let go of running last year, which is why I could now run again. We were both letting go of work and letting go of being defined by it in any way. Just before our sea experience we had been talking about this, exploring together what it meant to truly surrender and let our gifts take us where they would.

I had let go again today. I knew that I wanted to live and that I was prepared to fight for my life, but I also fully faced that we were in real danger and that we might not survive. It felt like some sort of an initiation of near-death experiences and now I felt freer than ever.

Day 220: Tues 17th December. *I was even more deeply committed to simply working with stuff: clearing, clearing, clearing*

I had stopped trying to self-actualise through running, to allow my ego to drive to be seen, to impress, to be important or OK through running. Now the Zen of running let the running take me where it would, becoming running rather than the runner. I trusted that all was unfolding as it should. I had let go of trying to control my destiny in any way and I was even more deeply committed to simply working with stuff: clearing, clearing, clearing.

Understanding the Process: Clearing

If we are clear then our true soul path will open up before us. We cannot make anything happen that is not going to happen and we cannot stop anything happening that is going to happen. This is our true destiny. However, the ego can play out many scenarios and take us totally away from our soul's purpose.

The id, ego, and super-ego are the three parts of the psychic apparatus defined in Sigmund Freud's structural model of the psyche. They are the three theoretical constructs in terms of whose activity and interaction our mental life is described.

According to this model of the psyche, the id is the set of uncoordinated instinctual trends; the super-ego plays the critical and moralising role; and the ego is the organised, realistic part that mediates between the desires of the id and the super-ego.

The super-ego can stop one from doing certain things that one's id may want to do. I use the term ego to relate to getting stuck in the mental patterns of our conditioning, resisting going into a place within to feel and listen to some deeper place of connection where it is possible to de-construct the way we have 'made ourselves up' and instead truly be ourselves.

Once we start to clear, then we see these experiences for what they are and that there is nothing to do but surrender.

To know all that we must learn to live is to let it all go, everything as we know it on this physical plane alongside fully living and embracing the moment. Being fully conscious is about letting go, of everything; more than simply knowing that everything is an illusion, everything a chimera, samsara; more than knowing it, is truly letting go of everything.

Anadi and I had explored this on our runs, our bodies so fit and able to run for miles. We had talked about how to be in relationship with our own bodies through stretching them to be fit and healthy and able, and in relationship with this beautiful planet that we live on and with one another. We ran in the sun, breathing hard, becoming one with the earth beneath us and the sky and the sun above us. We ran, we talked, and we shared in this human experience.

So alive, we explored our dying and how could we embrace this now so that we might fully live each moment: here, now. To fully live is to learn how to let go. Being in the sea was an ultimate metaphor for this.

Anadi's Perspective

As we grow up we can experience times when we are told we are wrong or not good enough. This can lead to us developing 'adaptations'. An adaptation can be something like 'I don't want to be wrong, or feel or be told I am wrong, as it makes me feel unloved or unwanted. I am going to do what is expected of me so I am right and loved'. This can lead to us creating all sorts of patterns and behaviours that take us away from our true selves, as we adapt to fit in with those around us.

One of my adaptations was to withdraw when confronted. As a child I hated being told I was wrong and I hated confrontation, and I would withdraw so no one could touch me. It was my way of not listening and saying 'F**k off' to the adults. 'You can shout all you want but I am not listening!' One of Julia's adaptations was to keep pushing if she felt she had not been heard or understood.

Both Julia and my adaptations were complimentary, they dovetailed like Ying and Yang. Because of this they were fertile ground for growth, investigation and, of course, in the negative: an out and out battleground. Fortunately, Julia and I had agreed to work everything out and so we were able use our adaptations for growth and clearing. The key was to recognise when I was withdrawing or Julia was pushing, as both of our behaviours were born of us feeling unheard.

An example of this was Julia casually mentioning that I had not read one of her previous books: *Running To Learn*. I replied that I hadn't had time. Julia said something along the lines of, 'Oh I don't mind you hadn't read it but if you had wanted to you would have made the time'. I replied, saying 'I have been busy'. Julia repeated that I had eighteen months in which to read it, she didn't mind I hadn't read it, but of course there was time. We then both dug in and played out our complimentary adaptations:

Julia pushing to make her point and me withdrawing in the way I had when I was a child. We both stopped before this turned into a silly argument, recognising our adaptations, and cleared what had come up for us. This is a perfect example of how something ridiculous can play out into to something that can break connection and relationship.

Once these patterns are recognised we can stop them before they start. We have the opportunity to handle the situation in a different way. This breaks the old pattern and it also allows us to feel safe with our partner and safe to express ourselves more truthfully. The above situation could not arise again: I do not withdraw, and Julia feels safer because I say what I mean. Julia has no need to push to feel heard and the wound in each of us is healed.

A Girlfriend for a Year Diaries: Part Nine

Day 224: Saturday 21st December. *The process of the past few days clearing and cleansing was deep within us both*

Today, we did laps past the house so that we could rehydrate as we ran. We ran alongside the river, through the jungle in the shady trees. We heard a crocodile snapping its jaws. Then we headed out into the direct sun and ran our beach lap to the point, and then back to the shade of the jungle to finish. We sweated and drank and became depleted and silent. The process of the past few days clearing and cleansing was deep within us both.

Day 225: Sunday 22nd December. *Our relationship brought to mind of the snakes on the path we kept seeing here — we were shedding skins*

This morning, our rest day from running, Anadi and I started the day with awesome sex, before coffee by the pool.

I'd had a conversation with my friend Simon, a traveller who lives abroad in the tropics and was in São Paulo. We'd exchanged our news and he'd asked how Anadi and I had adjusted to the climate. I'd told him about our routine.

'It's great you are exercising,' he said. 'Westerners often wilt and do very little under the heat and then can't sleep. Your way means you will get tired and go to bed early and sleep well'.
'We are sleeping well,' I'd said. 'But it's not great for our sex life!'
'Oh yes,' he'd said. 'You have to do it in the morning – if you get within half an hour of bedtime you'll be out like a light.' And so we followed his advice.

We had planned to walk to Porqueno, a restaurant that had been recommended to us by a women in Dominical who said she'd seen us running everywhere'. The walk took us an hour or so along the river. As we walked, we sang Christmas carols, the sun beating down on us, and sweat running off us. We reached the beach we ran on every day and walked along it and up the path through the woods to the door of Porqueno. It was run by a Canadian couple, Shelley and Jo, and the food they served us was delicious. We sat for five hours drinking freshly-squeezed juices and eating home-cooked food looking out at an exquisite ocean view. Yesterday we had run 20 miles, and today we needed to recover. The run yesterday felt like a distant dream. We had a perfect Sunday, eating and chatting.

Anadi was facing his own issues though. His business partner's initial enthusiasm for selling the business had waned, though Anadi was still keen to explore the idea – which led to conflict. On Dec 18th they'd had a conversation that totally changed the direction of the company and ended both their business partnership and friendship. The conversation spiralled out of control as Anadi's business partner didn't get his own way and proverbially 'threw his toys out of the pram', threatening to turn off the servers. Anadi stayed still within the interaction. An hour later an email came through from his business partner, whose wife had reminded him they still hadn't bought their children Christmas presents, and the pair of them had put in too much hard work to throw it all away. They had: the idea had been conceived 18 months ago and they had worked tirelessly on their dream.

In witnessing Anadi's shift from being 'controlled' by his partner – he has always kept the peace – I saw reflected there my adaptation with the controlling people in my life. Our relationship brought to mind of the snakes on the path we kept seeing here – we were shedding skins. Our old adaptations were well and truly done. Watching and being alongside Anadi as he was experiencing his partner's behaviour showed me that Anadi's 'stuff' had been in staying in the relationship in the first place, in 'trying to keep the peace' and not fully seeing the issues.

I experienced a strange parallel with his experience after reconnecting with an old friend, Gav, one of the group from Haslemere Border Athletics Club – my first ever club. He knew nothing of why I had left – he thought I had just 'done a runner'. And so I told him my story: I told him of Tim's treatment of me. In response he shared with me his own experience of his time with Tim and his adulation for him. In reading his account, something in me freed. I experienced a complete paradigm shift. I saw things about my past so much more clearly and let go to another level.

That night, Anadi and I drank a beer before our supper, then felt that another one was needed. After our meal we went to bed at 7.50pm, and rather than lying and chatting and making love as we had intended, we awoke the next morning at 5.30am having slept soundly for almost ten hours!

Day 228: Weds 25th December. Christmas Day. *'I know we will always be together' I said*

We had arrived on Christmas Eve to Hotel Cuna del Angel. We had got here very hot, tired, sweaty and dehydrated from a long run a few days ago and been served fresh fruit and drinks by the breakfast waiter – the warm welcome we had been given, coupled by the tranquillity and beauty of the hotel, had prompted Anadi to book us in for a special Christmas. All the rooms are called after Angels, each one watching over us for our stay. Our angel was called Barakiel, which means 'God's blessing'. Barakiel loves the forest and loves laughter.

We woke at 5.17 on Christmas morning to a sound like something out of Jurassic Park. We both quickly dressed and crept outside, to find the night watchman recording the noise on his iPhone.

'What is it?' we whispered.

'Monkeys' he replied.

We stayed listening in awe and after a while slipped back to our room. Now wide awake at 5.40 on Christmas morning, we decided to call our families before setting off for a Christmas adventure.

The lady on the reception desk looked us over as we asked the way to run to the beach and said, 'You look fit and used to exercise. If you like to explore, that path will take you to the sea.' adding the warning, 'But it is steep.'

We headed off and, after running for a while, found ourselves on a grassy plain. We could see the sea below, but no route to get there. We decided we'd missed a turning and, backtracking, soon found a steep rocky path to our left which had a faded sign beside it saying 'Playa'. The path took us right through the jungle with the trees reaching high into the sky. We clambered down rich red ridges of earth like steps until we reached a small secluded bay. No one was about, so we took off our clothes and dived into the ocean.

It was a magical bay, with lush scenery around us. The Pacific sparkled into the distance and we swam freely in the warm clear blue sea. After our swim, we sat naked on a log to dry, then put our clothes back on to make our way back to the hotel for breakfast.

As we made our way back up the path, there was suddenly a lot of noise above. Looking up, we saw monkeys everywhere – at least fifteen of them, their white faces looking down at us as they jumped from tree to tree all around. I felt vulnerable and a bit afraid.

'Keep moving,' Anadi said, and so I did, and after a while they started to jump away from us and carried on their way through their trees.

We spent a blissful Christmas Day in Cuna del Angel, lying in the shade on the grass, lunching on delicious bruschetta and fresh salad. As the sun faded, I suggested we go back to our magical bay. We sat there for quite a while (clothes on this time!), watching the sun set over the sea.

Not wanting to be in the jungle with night falling, I suggested we make our way back. As I took a step up the path, a long snake whipped across the path in front of me. Fear shot through my being! But the snake was gone in a flash and my fear faded as it vanished into the undergrowth. Over dinner, when we described the snake to our waiter, he told us that it was one of the most dangerous snakes in Costa Rica.

We had a magical dinner al fresco in the restaurant, with twinkling lights all around us. Our waiter was the same one who had saved us when we appeared at the top of the steps two weeks ago. We were pleased to see him, and he was glad to see us again. We told him he truly was our angel and that his friendly greeting to 'two sweaty castaways had meant that we wanted to return again to the cradle of the angel.

We were drinking our after-dinner coffee and talking about things we 'know'. I was saying that I had never really 'made' things happen – that I had instead always been committed to clearing my stuff, and to healing my wounds, then following my heart and my inner voice wherever that had directed, which had opened me to my life.

'What do you know now?' Anadi asked me.

'I know we will always be together' I said.

'Do you?'

'I wouldn't be here, doing this with you, if I don't know that' I had replied.

'Will you marry me?' He asked me.
I smiled. A lot.
'Yes, I will' I replied…

Day 231: Sat 28th December. *She was so happy for us both*

On Boxing Day, we woke up engaged to one another. We called Anadi's Mum and she became the first person to know: It felt important to Anadi to tell her first. It was the first time I had spoken to Anadi's mother;. We'd tried on Christmas Day, but she could hardly hear us – I guess the internet was too busy – but today, we spoke and she was so happy for us both. I liked talking to her. I felt it was important that I let my sister and brother know. Rosy was delighted. Stu was impossible to get hold of so I left him voicemails on all his phones.

Day 233: Monday 30th December. *The road less travelled beckoned us to follow it to wherever we were going*

We arrived in San Jose after an interesting journey! We had a taxi booked for 10am from our apartment. We left it spotless, far cleaner and brighter than when we arrived, and the dark energy that had lurked in the kitchen and the back bedroom when we arrived was gone.

At one minute past ten Anadi said I've had an intuition all morning that our taxi isn't coming.'

'Okay, I said. Let's get going.'

We had the mile along the rocky road to walk to Tortilla Flats, our favourite restaurant on the edge of the ocean, where we could catch the 10.30 bus to San Jose.

I changed out of my bra and top and put on a sports crop top in anticipation of the pouring sweat that a walk with heavy bags in the heat would engender, and off we went. We walked fast and covered the mile in twenty minutes. We were soaked in sweat, but we had made it in time.

Our bus didn't show. I called Amy for help – of course! At 10.50 it arrived and we had just piled onto it when Amy called back. It was really lovely to have a chat, as if we were up the road from each other, rather than 5,000 miles away. We travelled with four others: Tom from North Carolina, Rick from Texas, and Andes and Karen from Denmark. We stopped halfway for a loo break, and walked over the bridge to look at crocodiles basking in the river, some big crocs and a little one on the bank.

Our journey to the hotel took a lot longer than our journey to Dominical – five hours – in part because our driver got muddled as to which hotel we were staying and took us about 15 miles the wrong direction. Luckily, Amy saved the day by texting us a photo of the hotel we were bound for.

We arrived at the Marriott and were happy to be in the space between. We had lunch, then checked ourselves onto our flight. I was physically declining, with random sneezing and a runny nose that Anadi and I had had since Christmas Day. I had a shower, but was going downhill. Anadi made me a Lemsip and we lay on the bed together; it was 8.30pm.

At 11.30pm we woke up, brushed our teeth and fell into bed without supper.

The days since Christmas Eve had been amazing. The warmth, support and love we had been shown has been awesome. Many, many people had been celebrating online with us our public commitment to one another, loving it that we loved one another.

Anadi and I spoke on our last night in Dominical about how our mutual fierce independence had to be surrendered, and had been surrendered, in our dependency on one another. Being in relationship is about being one, recognising that we are all one; and within this, knowing how to keep ourselves safe as human beings on a human journey. In a committed relationship lies the ultimate, the space where we can see and experience our wholeness and paradoxically reclaim ourselves within the surrender of ourselves to the other. It is when we have truly learnt how to be alone that we can be together, and Anadi and I had spent a lifetime dedicated to learning just this: bringing us to the space of togetherness we now found ourselves in – and me with a beautiful (temporary) engagement ring on my finger.

We ran along the beaches and swam in the sea over those last few days. We were both noticeably fitter. Shifts had occurred within us, and outside too; our bodies leaner, faster and stronger, our life together unfolding. As we packed our bags we fully acknowledged that we owned hardly anything. We were travelling with less baggage, physically and spiritually. The road less travelled beckoned us to follow it to wherever we were going.

Day 234: Tues 31st December. 19.54pm Dec 31st Costa Rica time/1.54am Jan 1st UK time. *We had become time travellers*

We had become time travellers, seeing the New Year in as we journeyed, landing in the UK when most of the first day of the New Year was done before going for a New Year drink! We relaxed at the airport hotel. The staff were so friendly, and remembered us from our last visit. The hotel and the airport were a gap, a space, a moment. We enjoyed the no man's land space between time zones and places. I said to Anadi – several times – that as I moved into 2014 I intended to take these two thoughts with me:

'If there is no enemy within then the enemy outside can do us no harm.'

And: 'Enjoy the next few moments'.

Day 236: Thursday 2nd January. *Anadi and I were enjoying our nomadic lifestyle, being at home wherever we were*

Travelling on the train from London to Eastbourne, we gazed out of the window at a significantly altered landscape from when we left here four weeks ago.

'Was there always a lake there?' Anadi enquired.

A man who was just about to get off the train, explained to him that there was a river there, and fields usually, but that the Christmas weather had changed everything.

We walked out of the station concourse to bright blue skies and fresh January air. The Sunshine Coast welcomed us back with sun and light, to our home for a few weeks while I reconnected with my clients face to face and settled into my lovely little 'Alice in Wonderland' room in the basement of my friend Fi's home. She had taken to calling me her 'room-mate'.

Anadi and I were enjoying our nomadic lifestyle, being at home wherever we were. Arriving in a town I had lived in for some years, and yet not having a home there, had the feeling of finding ourselves in a completely new land.

It reminded me of the haiku our friend Brioni wrote us when she heard of our engagement:

I don't need a house, nor I
said she. I am home
with you; you are home with me

Day 237: Wednesday 3rd January. *Welcome to the Sunshine Coast! 'Pura Vida'!*

This morning, getting ready to run, we realised we only had shorts with us, not my first choice for Eastbourne in winter. 'It'll be fine' I said…

We set off to run along the seafront, and ten minutes later we were experiencing all that Eastbourne seafront could offer us as a 'welcome home' on a January morning at 7am. We couldn't hear one another speak as we ran into a strong headwind, rain and then a finale of hail! Welcome to the Sunshine Coast! 'Pura Vida'!

Day 248: Tuesday 14th January. *The energy was building and I wanted to love every minute*

Today, we were running round the Hollow, and I said to Anadi that having our wedding celebration this June felt too soon. An amazing celebration was forming and building, the inner temple was the place, many people were already gathering: the energy was building and I wanted to love every minute. An event to celebrate in June 2015 would allow us time to plan and for it to build and grow and blossom into an amazing festival in the future. Anadi agreed with me. 'Let's get married alone next month then, when we're in St Lucia.' he said. 'It will be our own ceremony, and we can have the celebration another time'.

Day 249: Wednesday 15th January. *Our nomadic life was unfolding before us*

This evening, Anadi and I went to the beach with my crystal ball. It was rainy and wild and the sea was being pulled in amazing directions by a moon that was hiding behind the clouds. It was a full moon in cancer. Anadi and I have our moon in cancer so this was a big time for us.

We placed the crystal ball, with our symbol stuck on it, on the beach and waited for a wave to wash over it, then we faced one another with the sound of the waves crashing and swirling. We looked into one another and said: 'We have created a life of love and consciousness and we are totally supported in this.'

It had been an incredible month. From full moon to full moon, Anadi's business partnership and friendship was over, we were getting married and our nomadic life was unfolding before us.

Day 250: Thursday 16th January. *I found an amazing blue wedding dress – in just ten minutes*

I found an amazing blue wedding dress – in just ten minutes! I was meeting Jim for a coffee and suddenly thought of a shop in South Street. I raced in, saw a beautiful dress that looked equally beautiful on and raced out. I was only a few minutes late for coffee.

Day 251: Friday 17th January. *I felt still and happy within, but I was aware there was imbalance*

The days since we had arrived home had passed in a blur of work. Today was the first that I had no clients since our return. Each day was fulfilling,, and I was engaged and enjoying my clients, but in truth each day I woke up tired and longing for more time to sleep, more time to run, more time with Anadi, more time to write, and more time to be still: to wake up with the day stretching ahead without a plan. I felt still and happy within, but I was aware there was imbalance. I was also aware that Anadi and I were still in transition.

Anadi asked me to 'work' with him on some of his stuff, and so we spent a day exploring, on our run, over lunch and driving up to London. We then bought my engagement ring and Anadi's wedding ring. I chose a beautiful moonstone and he chose a wedding ring that fitted together from two parts.

Things were on the move within his business. He had moved on from his ex-partner and there was only a vestige of anger left to clear, an old pattern fading and dying as he expanded to his greatest power and his light was given permission to fully shine. He had connected with Rosy as his new accountant. Money had come in to him from an award. He had completed his software and it was making its way out into the world already.

Later, Amy and I met to plan the wedding. I'd looked for all the relevant documents needed to marry and my decree absolute was missing. I used to have a divorce file, but it vanished in all the clearing out. I called Divorce Online and set the process in motion to get another one. Meanwhile, I implemented a backup plan – Andy (my ex-husband) knew where his was.

Day 256: Weds 22nd January. *My week had cleared and I had more space for me*

Today, Anadi accepted an offer on his flat. I was suddenly not responsible for us financially and at the same time, magically, my week had cleared and I had more space for me. I chatted with my big brother: a close and connected conversation. I felt loved by him, and that he was genuinely happy that I was happy.

My friend Gemma came to supper and said, 'I think you should make a big global announcement'. So we announced our wedding date on Facebook. The response was enormous. We were told that we were inspiring, that we gave hope and that we were living the dream, our dream.

Every day I fell more deeply in love with Anadi – there were no limits, no boundaries, our souls soared together when we made love - which we had been doing less of than we truly wanted to in the last three weeks. Our connection felt ever-deeper when we did make love, but our lifestyle was not lending itself to giving us the time for the endless days of lovemaking and lying about naked we had in the beginning. We both said that we wanted to create a life of love and consciousness – and within that, certainly the time to include lots of lying about and making love too.

Day 257: Thursday 23rd January. *I was not going to make it as a girlfriend for a year*

Today, I ran with my friend Fi along the seafront, with the sound of the ocean beside us and the seagulls squawking. Living and being, and especially running by the sea and along a beach, fed my soul. I was almost born on a beach, a sunny beach in Africa, and Anadi and I had travelled together to many beaches in sunny climes. We had walked along them, swum in their seas, jumped through the waves that lap or crash on their shores and almost died together in their waters. We had run for many miles, sometimes easily and slowly along the sand, and sometimes fast, running intervals, back and forth: sweating, breathing hard, the sun on our backs, our legs and lungs burning, our bodies and minds learning and growing through the stretch, extending just beyond what we thought we could do.

When I was nine or ten my Dad buried me in the sand. My sister and I made sand castles together, guided to great things by our civil engineer father! I jumped off sand dunes, leaping out as far as I could, and later on in my teenage years, when running performance started to matter to me, I practised running hard up them with great intent.

I collected shells and skimmed stones, spent hours catching prawns in a little net and with my bare hands, sunbathed for hours, scrambled up rocks and body-surfed onto Cornish beaches. I had picnicked on beaches and partied as well, but never had I ever thought I would be getting married on a beach…

Amy planned our wedding. Anadi paid for it and we were to be married in a simple St Lucia beach ceremony on February

24th. We had written our own vows, chosen a couple of poems and decided on the music we wanted played We were all set to be man and wife. I was so excited, so looking forward to being married to Anadi. I was not going to make it as a girlfriend for a year! It only really dawned on me this week that I would become a wife on Day 289. So should my book end then, when I became a wife for the rest of my life? I decided to let the story unfold as it would.

Something deep had shifted within over the last week. Anadi and I had spent the weekend family visiting. The itinerary had been pretty full on, but it was happy. I feel very welcomed into his clan, accepted, loved and sure that they were truly happy that Anadi had found his twin flame.

Almost a year ago we went to a coffee shop together and wrote down what we saw ahead. It had more than come true, except for one thing. I had not yet achieved being able to do handstands on dry land, like I used to when I was young and practically lived upside down. That intention could roll over to another year...

Anadi and I spent the evening reviewing where we were going, which way our souls wanted to go and what called us.

Day 263: Wednesday 29th January. *'You won't need a divorce folder again,' Andy said*

This morning, I trained in the gym with Matt; I loved it so much! I had improved a lot. I jumped and leapt and did squats and chin-ups and core work too and I felt about 30 years old – in fact my spirit was remembering being 20 years old, but in truth my body was not quite there. It was remembering though, and enjoying the movement, the strength, the agility, the flexibility. All last year I worked on the restriction and pain in my left side, month after month after month, and now my body was freeing up and I was starting to move as I did in the past.

Anadi texted me to say that my decree absolute had arrived by special recorded delivery. I had arranged to meet Andy, my ex-husband today so that he could lend me his. I texted him immediately to say that I would still like to meet if he wanted, but as the courts had sent mine, there would be no need if he had other things to do.

Then it was time for my 'hen do' – an intimate affair with my best friend. Wends met me under the clock at Waterloo. She had forgotten the purple feather boa and 'bride to be' sash, which were still in the hall at her home. I must admit to feeling rather relieved to be wearing the imaginary version all day instead. We made our way in the freezing-cold, pouring rain to Soho, talking of times past: a history trip when we were 15, the most memorable part of the day being our first sighting of a 'girlie mag' on the train, then finding our way to Soho because we had heard it was a risqué area and we were intrigued as to what we would find.

Wendy and I spent the afternoon in a warm vibrant Turkish restaurant, eating and talking and drinking coffee. We eventually emerged into the dark, shiny streets, with the rain still falling at 6.30, and started to head for home. A number 73 bus to Victoria stopped beside us in Oxford Street and on a spur of the moment decision Wends and I hugged goodbye and I leapt aboard.

Andy texted me later on to say he would still like to meet, and we agreed on Bibendum at 7.30pm. We had often met here when we were friends before we married. Anadi met me there first at 6.30pm on his way back from a meeting. I suggested he stay to meet Andy, and texted Andy to let him know he'd be there. They met – 'handing over the baton,' I said, laughing.

Anadi left us and Andy and I had supper together. 'You won't need a divorce folder again,' Andy said later as we sat chatting over our supper and talking about our lives. We had a lovely evening together; I remembered why we were such close friends and how that progressed to a love affair. I saw too why it could never have worked in that form. I felt some sadness that because of our marriage we were now not in a position to engage in the friendship. I saw all of this as we sat and ate supper and chatted. He was very happy with his partner, with his whole life, with a baby on the way. It felt a good thing to have met him. But maybe we would never meet again.

Day 266: Saturday 1st February. *When we met, we were both a bit wrung out*

I worked from 8am until 8pm, finishing feeling fulfilled and enriched from the day but also drained. Anadi had heard from his ex-business-partner, which had thrown him into a bit of a process, and meant that when we met we were both a bit wrung out.

We went to a bar and ate mozzarella melts and drunk a Whiskito which went straight to our heads. Our dialogue spiralled after Anadi expressed some fury about his ex-partner, and I reacted to his anger and he reacted to me reacting.

We came home depleted, feeling rather sad and exhausted. When we lay in bed I expressed a rising terror of the pattern being the same as before: the hope of the love I'd always dreamed of proving to be an illusion.

Anadi told me afterwards that he was aware I was in my 'withdrawing pattern', which threw up fear for him. He truly stayed in his body with the feelings; and said this was new, it changed everything. He had understood it intellectually before and always worked through things with me and saw his adaptation after he'd 'acted it out' – but now he really and truly felt it at the time it was happening. He worked with it and shared with me what was going on for him. Eventually we slept.

Day 268: Monday 3rd February. *I drove home feeling so uplifted in my heart to have connected so deeply with my sister*

Today, I met my sister for breakfast. As an accountant with her own business, this Monday was a celebration of the end of her massive January stint. Rosy and I are like twins, we know things about one another and we tend to do things at the same time; often big shifts occur together. Sisters connect in mysterious ways.

'I want to row,' she said, and told me about a woman she had met at an indoor rowing competition who is a top rower for her age group, the over 55s. Her husband had said to her, when the children had left home, that now it was her time and that she must do something for her. And so she rows.

Rosy said, 'I wish someone would say that to me.'

How I longed in that moment to be able to say that to my little sister. Instead I said, 'If Anadi's businesses do what they can, I will say that to you.'

We drank coffee, ate breakfast and found ourselves remembering the day that Mummy died. Rosy sat crying in the hotel dining room and I sat with her. 'At least we had each other,' she said. We then realised that the anniversary of her death was just three days away. I drove home feeling so uplifted in my heart to have connected so deeply with my sister.

240

Day 271: Thursday 6th February. *'Life's truest happiness is found in the friendships we make along the way'*

Today was my seventh betrothal anniversary – though not to Anadi! This date, apart from being the death day of my mother, is also the birthday of my sister-in-law Sue, and the date I met Simon and became betrothed. Seven years ago, Jane and Andrew and I had met in the Real Eating Company for our 'writing group'. I'd raced in late and Simon, the manager of the restaurant, came back and forth to us, to take an order we were never ready to place. I had just received my decree nisi and the elusive decree absolute was due in six weeks. I had divorced online and we were enjoying much hilarity as to the thought of my decree absolute being read out in a court in Swindon. Jane had imagined being able to be married in Swindon while being somewhere else entirely. I had said 'in six weeks I'll be free to marry again', to which Andrew replied, 'All the men will be hiding!' Jane and I, almost in unison, had said 'On the contrary, they will be queuing up!' At that moment Simon had appeared again to take our order. 'You'd marry me, wouldn't you' I asked him.

'Yes,' he replied.

'There – not a moment's hesitation!' said Jane.

And so it came to pass that Simon and I became 'betrothed' and each year the three of us travel to Lewes to meet and celebrate the betrothal, and pass our friendship plaque to the next person for the next year's safekeeping. The plaque reads thus: 'Life's truest happiness is found in the friendships we make along the way'.

Day 273: Sat 8th February. *Sharing laughter, food and memories*

Anadi and I ran to Leith Park in the morning. It was bright and cold, and the duck pond was still. The swans floated by as we ran around the circumference and up into the main park, around it and then home to shower and breakfast.

Rosy, Nick, Jamie and Jess arrived. It was Jamie's birthday. It was hard to believe that it had been seventeen years since I first sat looking at him in Rosy's arms, a tiny little baby.

The day passed in a delightful round of eating and talking, birthday cake and fizz with Stuart and the family; lunch in Pizza Express with Jamie and the Jeffery family; then more birthday cake for tea in our hotel, along with present opening before a wonderful occasion, a black tie dinner and dance to celebrate Sue and Stuart. It culminated with brunch the next day at their home, in a way a grand finale for seeing old friends, family members and being together, sharing laughter, food and memories.

After coming back from Edinburgh, I knew I had an enormous week of work ahead, but we were travelling to St Lucia, in the Caribbean, on Friday and so there was always light at the end of the tunnel.

Day 278: Thursday 13th February: *I felt energised and engaged, but needless to say, I hardly ran*

The week started with three clients on Monday night, and then I proceeded to work a twelve hour day on Tuesday, thirteen hours on Wednesday and fourteen hours on Thursday. I felt energised and engaged, but needless to say, I hardly ran.

At midnight, we drank a vodka and coke and exchanged our Valentine's cards and our vow.

'We have created a life of love and consciousness and we are totally supported in this.'

Apart from my wedding dress which Amy had packed for me, I had yet to pack anything, but after my long day of clients, bed seemed a better option. I arranged for a taxi to collect us at 6am and we set an alarm for 5am.

Day 279: Friday 14th February. *It felt a fitting gift for a soul pure in heart and intention*

I certainly needed the whole hour! I was just organised in time: packed, showered and dressed as the taxi called my phone to herald its arrival, whisking us towards the glorious island in the sun which was to become our home for three weeks and the place of our marriage.

The airport time was fun, and went so fast – as did the flight. We breakfasted in 'Eat'. After Anadi bought me my Valentine's present. I gave him a piece of rose quartz and a 'Lord of the Rings' ring:

One ring to rule them all,
One ring to find them,
One ring to bring them all,
And in the darkness bind them

It felt a fitting gift for a soul pure in heart and intention, who had no desire for any power over anyone.

We arrived at the Hewanorra airport in St Lucia twenty minutes ahead of schedule. But Anadi's bag did not appear.

We were a long time in the airport and emerged, still without a bag, to be greeted by Augustine who had patiently waited and was to drive us to our apartment.

243

We had a very enjoyable journey with him. He showed us the damage done by a storm that had hit St Lucia on Christmas Day and told us one story of a car that had been swept away in the torrents of wild water. Two men had died, but a six-year-old girl had survived. The girl said that a woman in white had come and lifted her out of the car and put her safely on dry land.

Augustine dropped us off at our apartment and, after a quick settle in – no unpacking for Anadi and I decided to leave unpacking until the morning – we followed the sounds of music and life to a street party that took place in Gros-Islet, where we were staying, every Friday evening.

We were hungry and a bit travel-weary, so we quickly chose a local restaurant and ordered chicken and rice and salad and a Margarita cocktail to celebrate our arrival on this beautiful isle - which we were to leave as husband and wife.

Day 280: Saturday 15th February: *'There is no fear in love; but perfect love casts out fear.'*

Lying about on our bed and talking meant that Anadi and I found ourselves deeply entwined and connected physically, our bodies relaxing again into the timelessness of speaking the language of love. Later, we wandered down the road to a café that served breakfast. Joanna made us strong black coffee and brought us glass after glass of ice cold water.

I told Anadi of a feeling I had in the night whilst sleeping, a feeling of being pinned down. I had felt afraid and so snapped back to consciousness. He said that this was the sign I wanted to leave my body to astral travel (one's energetic body leaving one's physical body whilst being completely aware that this happening). He had done this many times as a kid, but felt utterly terrified, catapulted out of his body into a vast space with entities flying about and no understanding of what was occurring. We made a pact that if one of us left our body, then we would call the other out, Anadi told me that it was easy to get out if someone called us.

Anadi and I wandered along the street today making our way to the seashore, which was about half a mile from where we were staying. We heard the sound of gospel music ringing out from a wooden building. The doors were open and the people inside were singing joyfully.

We walked up to the building and were reading the notice board that listed the days and times when the church services took place when a man came up to us, and invited us in. He showed us in and directed us to two spare seats, where we took our place amongst the regular congregation just as the minister was about to deliver his sermon.

'There is no fear in love; but perfect love casts out fear.'

He read from the Bible and this script from John's gospel is one that has always resonated with me. Anadi remembered that I had it written out and stuck it on my kitchen cupboard when we first met.

We sat in the church and let the words of the minister reverberate around us. The energy and good intention of the church, the rousing singing, the powerful prayer, the formal welcome for us: 'we would like to welcome our new friends'.

It was those words 'there is no fear in love; but perfect love casts out fear' more than any other spoken there today, that felt to be the reason we had been invited in and were sitting there together, just a week away from when we were to be married.

Day 281: Sunday 16th February. *We were ready to run*

This morning we wanted to run. 'I can run barefoot,' Anadi said, as his shoes had still not arrived! We had already established last night that my shorts fitted him (just) and I found a grey vest top which I pulled and stretched and ripped in the process. We were ready to run.

Anadi used to run barefoot in Trent Park. He mentioned this to me during the first conversation we ever had, and here he ran barefoot with me, wearing my clothes, along the coast road in St Lucia.

'Hey man, put some shoes on,' was the only comment he received.

We ran along the coast and the sun shone, the strong breeze was welcome. We ran down the street that we had walked though on Friday night, when we first arrived. The street was now becoming familiar to us. We walked to the supermarket down it; we walked to the seashore; we had even walked into a church on Saturday!

Day 282: Monday 17th February. *Now I was here in St Lucia, I could hardly wait to marry Anadi*

This morning we were awake by 5.40am and making love as the light filtered through and heralded another day in St Lucia. Having more time for sex again was awesome. After making love we drank coffee and decided to set off early on an adventure. We found our way over to the other side of the island, where a spectacular empty beach greeted us, then climbed up a steep track to the highest point we could find. We followed our noses and ended up back in the road that we had run along yesterday, six miles of running a perfect loop! We had the sea to keep us from wandering too far afield.

Now I was here in St Lucia, I could hardly wait to marry Anadi. Again, I felt that I had met my twin flame. I hadn't quite made being a girlfriend for a year. On February 24th – Day 289 of the 365 – I would marry Anadi on the beach and become a 'wife for life'. I found myself drawn to write about our lovemaking.

Magic and the art of making it with you

I love the sensations within my body as we lie together, our mouths together: kissing you my love, the one I love, your lips on mine, soft and yielding, open to me and to limitless love. I feel my body opening up to you and to the energy that flows between us and between my legs. I feel it moving in my thighs and in my heart; I feel warmth, heat, desire in my belly and in my being. Your tongue is touching mine, exploring my lips, my teeth, my mouth, igniting the heat I can feel within me, the heat of desire that turns deeper inward and I am falling into you, beyond the room and the bed we are lying on.

I see in your eyes the possibility of many worlds. As you enter me I can feel my body welcome you, possess you and so free you, yield to you. You are mine and I am yours, so deep, so wet, so soft, so hard.

You are within me and inside me totally. Warm skin on skin together connects, and we are as one; limbs, eyes, hands, your hardness in my wetness, thrusting then still then thrusting and we move together, as we journey deeper. We are kissing openly, passionately, eyes and tongues and minds linked and locked together; we are one, we have the key.

Your hand moves on the inside of my thigh. Can we be any closer than we are right now in this moment, with our bodies pressed together: heat, sweat, lust, love, magical desire expressing pure love.

My body wants to come, to feel the power of the energy deep in my being, But I want this to last forever, heart to heart, you moving in me, you in me forever, the smell of sex, the language of love. And so I hold the energy that is building and radiating in my being, from me and through you, because I want this to last forever.

Time is suspended and we are breathing, looking, fucking into one another. My body opens, it asks that I surrender to love, to you, to our

248

> *dance and let this energy move. In that same moment I want this to last forever.*
>
> *Breathing together, we are close, to love, to the energy, to pure consciousness, to the release and the coming, the connection, an ending and a beginning always; death, life and love in the same flow; sweat and love and radiating joy.*
>
> *Our mouths are wet and so is my back with sweat. Sweat is dripping from your hair onto my face, your eyes in mine, your mouth on mine, you in me. Our breathing is deep with desire, deep with the ecstasy of our connection, of sex, of the rising energy. We are rising in love.*
>
> *'I'm going to come in you.' My energy moves to those words as you fill me. Your body moves in mine and my being lets go into the ecstasy of the pure magic of fucking, loving, joining, making it with you.*

Later, we had a deeper 'process' that took us to know ourselves even more fully. Over coffee we started to explore our life, our intentions, and how we wanted to live out being Anadi and Julia on this planet. The life we were creating of love and consciousness – how did it look?

It was fun to do, affirming our paths: our relationship central to everything and our work coming from this, along with all other aspects that came from within us – running, writing, music, relationships with friends and family. The process occurred as we wrote and talked and it became apparent how precarious our life is in human terms, how little security we had in terms of definite income or stability in material terms. It accessed some fear to be released, which made us tired and so, soon after we had eaten later on in the apartment, we fell into bed and quickly to sleep.

Day 283: Tuesday 18th February. *There had been an earthquake in Martinique and we had experienced the tremor*

We woke today at 5.27am, to the sound of the cockerel crowing, which had already become part of the fabric of our new life. We were lying curled up into one another when suddenly the bed started to shake and then the whole house was shaking. It was when I heard what sounded like a cracking noise in the ceiling that I leapt up.

'We have to get out, we have to get out!'

'I'm not sure that's the best thing' Anadi said...

It stopped very soon and so we put the kettle on for coffee.

Looking for news half an hour later while we sat in the balcony drinking the coffee, we found that there had been an earthquake in Martinique and we had experienced the tremor. An email from Amy in response to mine telling of the tremor, reminded us that we deeply experienced the water element in Costa Rica – being dragged out by the rip tide, the power of the ocean - and now we felt the earth shaking beneath us. Anadi and I reflected that we had been affected by fire in Santorini with the main electricity generator being burnt out just as we arrived on the island, and in Morocco the air element: at high altitude, we were at times suspended in thin air. The fifth element is the void: nothingness, consciousness. We are that, we are nothing, we are the void and love is the life we have created and are supported in.

We had both woken up feeling clear and the earth tremor shook any vestiges of our 'stuff' out. We ran to the road that leads to Pigeon Island. We later learnt from Fenella, our wedding planner, that we were to be married in the very park we ran through. We ran intervals of 20 x 1 minute all along that road, with the ocean lapping beside us and the sun rising higher in the sky. Having not done intervals since we were in Costa Rica, I felt them a bit. But, as Anadi said, when he has a programming puzzle to work out, it challenged him to use his special gifts to create platforms that were unbreakable and that really worked. I put a race ahead of me so that I could unravel the knots and find ways to run free and in so doing strip off anything that lay between me, myself and truth.

As we walked back after our interval training the rain started to fall. We kept walking as the rain became heavier and saw a man dancing with abandon in the street. We walked, he danced and people sheltered until the rain blew away from the little island in the sun.

I enjoyed taking in the sights and sound of the island. The steel band was practising all morning: 'When the Saints Go Marching In'. The rain came down three times – no wonder the island was so lush, green and verdant. A street vendor sat behind her trestle tables laden with bananas, coconuts and potatoes.

We met with Fenella to go over final details and sign necessary legal documents, and were all set to go. She spoke of her seven year old daughter who loves to run: 'She runs everywhere, she doesn't walk, she just wants to run'. I told her that the moment I could walk, I ran: that I ran everywhere and how on family walks because I would not walk. My father used to say, 'Run to that tree, and then back to us. Now ran to that bush... Now that tree...' This way, everyone was happy. I suggested that maybe she tried the same thing with her little running daughter.

Later, Anadi spoke of the shift he had experienced since his business partner 'process'. He deeply felt that it had helped him create unbreakable platforms. The creativity and power that came from within him for this, was exactly the same energy, and from the same position, that he was able to create his businesses, and our lifestyle. This process set him free. And me too. It demonstrated the trust in our connection to ourselves, consciousness and our own unique expression in human form while on this planet.

Day 285: Wednesday 19th February. *There seemed no reason to us for it to be out of bounds*

Today, we explored Pigeon Island, jogging there slowly, as my body hurt. We paid our money to get in and ran up the first hill in the park. Reading the sign, I learned that it was heralded as one of the most important monuments of Saint Lucia's history: a living museum within a natural setting, contributing towards St Lucia's reputation as a 'paradise island. Its predominant features were the, 'two peaks, joined by a saddle, with a spur to the North East running into the sea.' And this is where we were to be married.

We ran up to the fortress and sat on the wall, chatting and looking across to Martinique. We then ran and scrambled up to the highest point and looked out over the ocean and the breathtaking views. Running down, we found some ropes across a path saying 'Out of Bounds', leading to a gazebo.

'Look,' Anadi said, joking, 'There's a sign saying entry for Julia and Anadi only'.

We lifted the rope up and dived under it, making our way along the rocky path that took us right to the water's edge before ending by a big rock face. There seemed no reason to us for it to be out of bounds.

We stopped for a bite to eat before making our way to look at the beach where we were to be married. It was packed with people and even though the lady on the desk at the entrance to the park assured us it wouldn't be like that on the day we were keen to find a more private spot. Standing under a little gazebo, in the out of bounds area, both of us had experienced the peaceful and still energy there. We had fallen in love with it.

I emailed Fenella on our return and, almost by return, she said that the gazebo was free on Monday and that she had emailed everyone to let them know of the change of venue.

So on Monday we would walk together up the paving stones that lead to the gazebo, and I would make my promise to Anadi, to always honour the beauty of his soul and to love him eternally and truly. On this beautiful island in the sun, he would take me to be his wife.

Day 286: Thursday 20th February. *Essentially, I was no longer attached to the story*

Today we woke at 6am, having slept well. After lovely sex and a meal out with two beers each, I felt totally relaxed and had fallen into a deep sleep the moment we'd arrived home. My muscles had responded well to the 'active rest' which I'd done earlier that evening and the beers had topped off the 'release'.

Having not felt it for months, my psoas muscle pain had kicked off again a couple of days ago. It is the muscle most associated with deep emotional and spiritual trauma, which made sense given that in three days I would no longer be a girlfriend for a year. All of my 'stuff' was associated and tangled up with my relationships with men and my running, which had been inextricably linked. Essentially, I was no longer attached to the story. However, my unconscious seemed to be suddenly afraid to go forward and was holding on, terrified.

We breakfasted at Joanna's, then had a deep tissue massage at the marina. I also had a manicure. This unusual occurrence, coupled with me trying to avoid tan lines by walking about with my vest made into a strapless top was as close as I had come to turning into 'Bridezilla'. I was even persuaded to go for blue sparkly nails to match my blue wedding dress. However, after agreeing to having my hair up for the wedding, it proved to be a step too far and I ended up cancelling my appointment.

I then had a session with a client on the phone. I enjoyed talking with them and afterwards felt in need of something light to eat before we went running. I also wanted to see how my psoas was doing. I left Anadi writing an email and jogged up the road, noticing that my body was much improved.

The supermarket had not yet opened and so I was hesitating.

'Can I help you?' enquired a woman holding a baby.

'I need some milk' I said.

'Go right down that road and right again' she said, pointing left.

I clarified a couple of times but she said the same thing and pointed the same way, so I ran down the road. At the end, a man in a car saw that I was unsure about which way to turn, wound his window down and directed me to turn left where I found a tiny shop with milk, biscuits and some freshly made fairy cakes. I told the woman who served me that Anadi and I were getting married on Monday and she said, 'May God's blessing be on you both'.

Later we brunched in Ole before I returned home for another client. Our day finished with the street party, which we had been to last week the moment we arrived. We had been here a week already! We wandered through the streets packed with people dancing, eating and drinking, and loud music playing from various sound systems as we passed by. The smell of home-cooked food filled the air, with the occasional waft of cannabis as we neared the beach.

We stopped at one stall where a local woman had prepared vast vats of banana salad, chicken legs and macaroni cheese. She piled our plates high and we sat at a plastic trestle table covered in a bright red cloth and ate our supper, with company from a semi-circle of skinny cats at our feet waiting for pickings. We stopped in a bar and ordered rum cocktails, which were delicious.

Day 287: Fri 21st February 2013. *I felt happy to have crossed the bridge into the world and the heart of a people I did not know at all*

It was 35 years since St Lucia attained full independence today, and was is a public holiday. Last night the Friday night street party here in Gros-Islet had been particularly lively, heralding the day of celebrations to come. This morning, with the feeling of the cocktails still in our bodies, we drank coffee on our balcony, filled up on water and stoically set off to run to Castries, the capital of the island. Our bodies warmed into the run as the road wound its way to the city. We stopped off on a beach on the way and watched the locals playing beach volleyball by the water's edge.

Arriving at Castries six miles away, hungry for some breakfast, we found the town shut for business and open for more partying in the street. We bought a bottle of water and wandered though the throngs and inadvertently into some quiet streets, happening upon a group of guys sitting around together. One of them started to follow us. 'Where you going? You want some Sensi? It's good stuff... We give you a free smoke...' We thanked him, but said no thanks and soon emerged again onto the busier streets to find a bar selling beer and coca cola. With no food in us as yet we chose the coke and made a plan to find a taxi and head home for food.

A guy in a van, with another man in the passenger seat stopped beside us. 'You want a ride; I will show you the island.'

'We want food!' I said.

'I will show you some countryside and take you to my home and give you food and then take you back to Gros-Islet,' he said. 'For 60 US dollars'. Anadi looked at me.

'Let's do it,' I said.

'We'll give you 50 dollars' Anadi said, 'and you have a deal'.

We clambered into the van and Christopher and 'the Doc' introduced themselves. They drove us high into the hills, with awesome views of the lush countryside all around us. After a few miles, he pulled over to a stall where there were two men talking together and a woman with a machete was expertly making chops out of a recently slayed pig. They spoke Creole to each other and ignored Anadi and I. It was like we were ghosts.

Christopher bought some meat, along with a delicacy for us to eat, like big juicy sausages, which they cut into smaller pieces. They were very spicy and rich, we made appreciative noises. The woman engaged with us then, smiling and nodding with us at our appreciation.

'What is it made of?' Anadi asked her.

'Blood and onions' she replied.

I was glad not to have known before sampling the 'pudding', as they called it.

We clambered back into the van and soon arrived at a steep rocky track that lead us down to a community of houses: a place called Babonneau, right in the middle of the island. Christopher's sister Tine welcomed us, introducing us to her cousin and youngest daughter, then her husband 'Davy Crockett' who shook our hands and did a little dance before disappearing to prepare us food.

Vera and Tine showed us around. Tine was a keen gardener. and we stood amongst the plants she loved so much.

'I love the plants more than him' she told us, gesturing inside to her partner preparing lunch.

'He loves you and you love the plants, it works,' I said, and they all laughed.

By this time, we were sitting in front of the house eating a plate of chicken with wild yam and plantain, and orange squash to drink. Another cousin, had appeared and the houses of many more relations had been pointed out to us.

Having shared with them that Anadi and I were about to be married, Tine brought me a photo album to show me the wedding photos of her second daughter Sharmain, who married an Irish man five years before and now lived in Belfast. While we were looking at the photos, Sharmain coincidently phoned her Mum, who immediately handed the phone to me, and so I told her I was sitting in her mother's home looking at photos of her.

Christopher brought us home eventually, driving us back on a different route. We climbed high, and saw the island in glorious relief; then landed back in Gros-Islet, with a little more of the island in our veins, somewhat changed by our connection to the people here: a little more St Lucian than we were before. Yet there was a history and a culture ingrained, so even within feeling connected at the heart and soul level to our hosts and hostesses, I was also aware of the differences between us. I felt happy to have crossed the bridge into the world and the heart of a people I did not know at all.

It is through crossing the bridge into one another's worlds, and through validating and seeking to understand one another, that we can all become more whole, interaction by interaction, through connecting authentically with each other.

Day 289: Sunday 23rd February. *'I wonder which of you will have da shakin' legs'*

Today Anadi and I went to have breakfast at Joanna's, and she gave us a special breakfast with extra coffee and special bread to celebrate our marriage the following day. It was two weeks since she had first made us breakfast, when we wandered in on our first morning here looking for food. Anadi was still wearing the clothes he had travelled in, his bag having gone on its own journey to Trinidad.

'I wonder which of you will have da shakin' legs,' she said.

Anadi and I were pretty sure that neither of us would have the shaking legs. How wrong we were, as we both found out next morning!

Day 290: Monday 24th February. *My love for you is without beginning and without end*

I decided that a run with some half miles 'at pace' would be a good cure for our nerves! Anadi was not so sure about this, but he gamely set off with me through the village that has become our home in the past two weeks. In fact, to marry here, we had to officially be residents, which actually only meant two days of being on the island, but Gros-Islet *had* become our new home. Castro, who owned the guest house we were staying in, said to Anadi the other day: 'it's good to see you are happy, running around everywhere. Stay in St Lucia, don't go back.'

So we set off in the morning, running through our village, our new home, to the sea. After running along the seashore for a while, I announced the first half-mile repetition would be commencing. Our shaking legs relaxed and became slightly tired legs instead, and we returned to our apartment with less butterflies in our tummies.

Our day progressed like a usual Monday. We went for brunch in Ole, one of our favourite eateries at the marina, where we chatted with our waitress and watched the boats sailing on the blue sea. After brunch, we walked home to get ready. Anadi bathed and shaved and I did a little meditation on the floor; then

I had a bath and did my hair, simply washing it, drying it and putting a glittery hair band in. Then I came to putting on my blue dress, at which point I realised it had been a mistake to 'do' my hair first. Anadi helped me wriggle into my dress, which would only go on over my head. My hair needed to be 'done' again, the car was arriving in five minutes, and I was certainly challenged to stay present and in the moment.

Augustine, who had collected us from the airport ten days before, was waiting for us in his smart chauffeur clothes, and we clambered into the back of the sleek white wedding car in our smart wedding clothes. There were no shaking legs at all now.

Hours previously, we had run along the same road. We had relaxed as we ran and the mantra from the book *Born to Run*, of, 'Easy, light, smooth, fast', echoed in my head. Now, we drove the same route and we felt light and at ease as the car sped along smooth and fast. Our marriage was minutes away.

We arrived and climbed out of the car to be greeted by Fenella, and Dani our photographer. Anadi and I walked together up the paving slabs to the gazebo where Lesley, who was marrying us, read to us the love recital from *The Prophet* by Kahil Gibram. He read us the whole passage; at the exact time, I later discovered, that over 5,000 miles away in England, our dear friend Jane was reading the same passage out loud to us.

He finished the reading I loved so much, then married us. Anadi and I had created our own ceremony and we finished with words we had written especially for one another.

Anadi said:

In your eyes I have found my home,
In your heart I have found true love,
In your soul I have found my twin flame,
With you I am whole
My love for you is without beginning and without end.

259

I replied:

I love you
I love you with all of my heart
I love you with all of my being
You have shown me by being yourself
That what I have always known is possible in love
Is not a dream but the truth
I will always honour the beauty of your soul
And love you eternally and truly my twin flame.

And, then I was married to my twin flame, feeling so happy that we had eventually found one another.

Understanding the Process:
Never Stop Shining

Like many things in life, there is more fun to be had when we have put hard work and hours of practice in, and got ourselves to a stage to really enjoy them. This is the same for anything, whether playing a musical instrument, becoming proficient at a sport or learning a profession or a physical practice or an art.

It is the same in relationship. The skills needed to clear our stuff so that we can truly relate with one another is as much a skill as anything else that we desire to enjoy doing – and to enjoy doing well, so that it appears effortless and natural, even easy!

Anadi and I have been told that our relationship inspires and even 'gives hope for the happily ever after'. In some ways this is why I have written this book, because otherwise it is a bit like a romantic film, where boy and girl kiss and the film ends with a happily ever after dream, easy as that.

It's not as easy as that! There is a personal process to true love, which I hope our relationship and this book inspires. If we are clear, then love is the natural state, and we can see that conflict and stress and separation is the aberration.

Often when people see Anadi and I, it is evident we have a deep love and a true connection. However, this has only been possible for us because of the years of 'core work' we have both done on ourselves and the on-going work we do in our own relationship.

Our spirit remains the same – always – but it gets buried under 'stuff'. Shame and self-hatred then often lead the way, and so in not feeling loveable or OK at the deepest level, we become susceptible to projection and defensiveness in the face of our wounds being activated.

Anadi and I's connection was never in question – we fell in love very fast. But connection and love isn't always enough, as the heartbreak of many ended relationships demonstrates. The core work is about learning to love ourselves and allowing our spirit to shine through.

Boyfriend for a year: Anadi's epilogue...

What an amazing adventure! We have journeyed from uncertainty to being married! Who would have thought it: Mr Free Spirit marrying Miss Free Spirit. It feels like the adventure has just begun. We have cleared the way for something truly magnificent and I feel that is what this past fourteen months has been about – both of us clearing the way, both letting go of limitations and conditionings, of the social restrictions pulling us back from being the conscious and free spirited beings we obviously are.

To wholly be with Julia I have had to address the adaptations that protected me as a child, adaptations that would have me internalise my processes, not talking about what is going on because of a fear of being smashed or rejected. Adaptations that would ultimately lead me to disconnect from Julia, even in the smallest of ways. All this completely unconscious of course, and very difficult to face as they were deeply ingrained in my psyche. Adaptations that had more than passed their sell-by date and had to be cleared. These married up with Julia's fears of me exiting, not maintaining our connection and of me not being able to meet her fully. We were the perfect match! Fortunately Julia and I have been working on our stuff, our childhood wounds, our whole lives: both of us immovable from the path of clearing and freeing ourselves from any part of us not conscious.

My whole life has been described as that of a rebel. I never felt the need to follow the normal path of life expected by my family or society. The ultimate act of rebelling for me has been to free myself from rules that are not mine, to clear the unconscious patterns forced upon me when I had no choice and was unable to defend myself, to free the spirit I am and that has always wanted to soar and shine, unrestricted and completely connected to my soul path. Little did I know when I picked Julia up from the station I was going to meet my twin flame, another rare soul whose whole life has been dedicated to being conscious, free and unchained by the expectations of others.

So here we now are, our connection still deepening and rising more and more in love. This is possible only with both of us being thoroughly in every moment, watching for reactions in the body that come from past wounds and clearing, clearing, clearing!

I can say that the past fourteen months have taught me about relating at the deepest level: being clear of 'stuff' and knowing where my unconsciousness patterns are has allowed me to connect with Julia on levels far deeper than I ever imagined. Our intimacy, both in general life and during lovemaking continues to deepen, and there are no limits to our journeying together, both inner and outer.

In Corfu – a year on

Sept 15th 2014. I am sitting on the terrace in Stefanos Place in Corfu where we are 'living for now'. We arrived here exactly two weeks ago carrying with us our hand baggage and another bag each, holding our 20kg allowance. This is now all we own in the world.

We have done what was started just over a year ago in a conversation in Santorini. We are both working to create our new lives, our new businesses, which we can do from wherever we are in the world. I am looking out over the Ionian Sea which I swim in each day and the hills around me, which I am becoming familiar with running up! We feel free.

Acknowledgements

This book would not be a book without Simon Broad – thank you Si for crafting my story, my words, my thoughts, my stream of consciousness – you are a master craftsman and I love working with you so much.

Thank you to Amy Law-Smith for patiently and tirelessly and enthusiastically collecting all the pieces of writing as they emerged and collating something that Si could work with...!

Thank you to Athena Jane Churchill for my beautiful book jacket, and to Hannah Ahmed who worked with Jane to bring it to the book.

Thank you Jeremy Hemming for once again reading my words and proofreading every one, I salute you!

Thank you to Dani Devaux who photographed Anadi's and my wedding; it is her photo that has been used for the creation of the cover – Dani takes fabulous photos!

Thank you to Fiona McCready and Tim Crook and Stephanie Dunn and Amy and Anadi for reading a first draft! And for the time you took to make suggestions...

Thank you Emily Dubberley for your enthusiasm and support in setting this book in flight, for your energy and your expert eye...

Thank you to Ros Draper, my wonderful therapist and supervisor and inspiration always. Thank you for guiding me, for seeing me and my energy, for always believing in me and for teaching me about the Imago relationship theory and encouraging me to gain further training in it – concepts I have learned and applied echo in these pages...

And thank you Anadi for being willing to share our story with the world!

I love you all very much.